# CHILD ABUSE

# THE ENCYCLOPEDIA OF
# HEALTH

## PSYCHOLOGICAL DISORDERS AND THEIR TREATMENT

Solomon H. Snyder, M.D. · General Editor

# CHILD ABUSE

## William A. Check

Introduction by C. Everett Koop, M.D., Sc.D.
*Surgeon General, U.S. Public Health Service*

CHELSEA HOUSE PUBLISHERS
New York    Philadelphia

*The goal of the* ENCYCLOPEDIA OF HEALTH *is to provide general information in the ever-changing areas of physiology, psychology, and related medical issues. The titles in this series are not intended to take the place of the professional advice of a physician or other health-care professional.*

**Chelsea House Publishers**
EDITOR-IN-CHIEF  Nancy Toff
EXECUTIVE EDITOR  Remmel T. Nunn
MANAGING EDITOR  Karyn Gullen Browne
COPY CHIEF  Juliann Barbato
PICTURE EDITOR  Adrian G. Allen
ART DIRECTOR  Maria Epes
MANUFACTURING MANAGER  Gerald Levine

**The Encyclopedia of Health**
SENIOR EDITOR  Paula Edelson

**Staff for CHILD ABUSE**
ASSISTANT EDITOR  Laura Dolce
COPY EDITOR  Brian Sookram
DEPUTY COPY CHIEF  Nicole Bowen
EDITORIAL ASSISTANT  Jennifer Trachtenberg
PICTURE RESEARCHER  Nisa Rauschenberg
ASSISTANT ART DIRECTOR  Loraine Machlin
SENIOR DESIGNER  Marjorie Zaum
LAYOUT  Victoria Tomaselli
PRODUCTION COORDINATOR  Joseph Romano

3   5   7   9   8   6   4

Library of Congress Cataloging-in-Publication Data

Check, William A.
   CHILD ABUSE / William A. Check ; introduction by C. Everett Koop.
      p.   cm. — (The Encyclopedia of health. Psychological
disorders and their treatment)
   Bibliography: p.
   Includes index.
   Summary: Discusses the forms of child abuse, its historical and
cultural context, and society's methods of dealing with it.
   ISBN 0-7910-0043-5.
         0-7910-0509-7 (pbk.)
   1. Child abuse—United States—Juvenile literature.   2. Abused
children— Services for—United States—Juvenile literature.
[1. Child abuse.]   I. Title.   II. Series.          88-30164
HV6626.5.C47   1989                                  CIP
362.7'044—dc19                                        AC

# CONTENTS

# THE ENCYCLOPEDIA OF HEALTH

## THE HEALTHY BODY

The Circulatory System
Dental Health
The Digestive System
The Endocrine System
Exercise
Genetics & Heredity
The Human Body: An Overview
Hygiene
The Immune System
Memory & Learning
The Musculoskeletal System
The Neurological System
Nutrition
The Reproductive System
The Respiratory System
The Senses
Speech & Hearing
Sports Medicine
Vision
Vitamins & Minerals

## THE LIFE CYCLE

Adolescence
Adulthood
Aging
Childhood
Death & Dying
The Family
Friendship & Love
Pregnancy & Birth

## MEDICAL ISSUES

Careers in Health Care
Environmental Health
Folk Medicine
Health Care Delivery
Holistic Medicine
Medical Ethics
Medical Fakes & Frauds
Medical Technology
Medicine & the Law
Occupational Health
Public Health

## PSYCHOLOGICAL DISORDERS AND THEIR TREATMENT

Anxiety & Phobias
Child Abuse
Compulsive Behavior
Delinquency & Criminal Behavior
Depression
Diagnosing & Treating Mental Illness
Eating Habits & Disorders
Learning Disabilities
Mental Retardation
Personality Disorders
Schizophrenia
Stress Management
Suicide

## MEDICAL DISORDERS AND THEIR TREATMENT

AIDS
Allergies
Alzheimer's Disease
Arthritis
Birth Defects
Cancer
The Common Cold
Diabetes
First Aid & Emergency Medicine
Gynecological Disorders
Headaches
The Hospital
Kidney Disorders
Medical Diagnosis
The Mind-Body Connection
Mononucleosis and Other Infectious Diseases
Nuclear Medicine
Organ Transplants
Pain
Physical Handicaps
Poisons & Toxins
Prescription & OTC Drugs
Sexually Transmitted Diseases
Skin Disorders
Stroke & Heart Disease
Substance Abuse
Tropical Medicine

# PREVENTION AND EDUCATION: THE KEYS TO GOOD HEALTH

C. Everett Koop, M.D., Sc.D.
Surgeon General,
U.S. Public Health Service

The issue of health education has received particular attention in recent years because of the presence of AIDS in the news. But our response to this particular tragedy points up a number of broader issues that doctors, public health officials, educators, and the public face. In particular, it points up the necessity for sound health education for citizens of all ages.

Over the past 25 years this country has been able to bring about dramatic declines in the death rates for heart disease, stroke, accidents, and, for people under the age of 45, cancer. Today, Americans generally eat better and take better care of themselves than ever before. Thus, with the help of modern science and technology, they have a better chance of surviving serious—even catastrophic—illnesses. That's the good news.

But, like every phonograph record, there's a flip side, and one with special significance for young adults. According to a report issued in 1979 by Dr. Julius Richmond, my predecessor as Surgeon General, Americans aged 15 to 24 had a higher death rate in 1979 than they did 20 years earlier. The causes: violent death and injury, alcohol and drug abuse, unwanted pregnancies, and sexually transmitted diseases. Adolescents are particularly vulnerable, because they are beginning to explore their own sexuality and perhaps to experiment with drugs. The need for educating young people is critical, and the price of neglect is high.

Yet even for the population as a whole, our health is still far from what it could be. Why? A 1974 Canadian government report attributed all death and disease to four broad elements: inadequacies in the health-care system, behavioral factors or unhealthy life-styles, environmental hazards, and human biological factors.

To be sure, there are diseases that are still beyond the control of even our advanced medical knowledge and techniques. And despite yearnings that are as old as the human race itself, there is no "fountain of youth" to ward off aging and death. Still, there is a solution to many of the problems that undermine sound health. In a word, that solution is prevention. Prevention, which includes health promotion and education, saves lives, improves the quality of life, and, in the long run, saves money.

In the United States, organized public health activities and preventive medicine have a long history. Important milestones include the improvement of sanitary procedures and the development of pasteurized milk in the late 19th century, and the introduction in the mid-20th century of effective vaccines against polio, measles, German measles, mumps, and other once-rampant diseases. Internationally, organized public health efforts began on a wide-scale basis with the International Sanitary Conference of 1851, to which 12 nations sent representatives. The World Health Organization, founded in 1948, continues these efforts under the aegis of the United Nations, with particular emphasis on combatting communicable diseases and the training of health-care workers.

But despite these accomplishments, much remains to be done in the field of prevention. For too long, we have had a medical care system that is science- and technology-based, focused, essentially, on illness and mortality. It is now patently obvious that both the social and the economic costs of such a system are becoming insupportable.

Implementing prevention—and its corollaries, health education and promotion—is the job of several groups of people:

First, the medical and scientific professions need to continue basic scientific research, and here we are making considerable progress. But increased concern with prevention will also have a decided impact on how primary-care doctors practice medicine. With a shift to health-based rather than morbidity-based medicine, the role of the "new physician" will include a healthy dose of patient education.

Second, practitioners of the social and behavioral sciences—psychologists, economists, city planners—along with lawyers, business leaders, and government officials—must solve the practical and ethical dilemmas confronting us: poverty, crime, civil rights, literacy, education, employment, housing, sanitation, environmental protection, health care delivery systems, and so forth. All of these issues affect public health.

Third is the public at large. We'll consider that very important group in a moment.

Fourth, and the linchpin in this effort, is the public health profession—doctors, epidemiologists, teachers—who must harness the professional expertise of the first two groups and the common sense and cooperation of the third, the public. They must define the problems statistically and qualitatively and then help us set priorities for finding the solutions.

To a very large extent, improving those statistics is the responsibility of every individual. So let's consider more specifically what the role of the individual should be and why health education is so important to that role. First, and most obviously, individuals can protect themselves from illness and injury and thus minimize their need for professional medical care. They can eat a nutritious diet, get adequate exercise, avoid tobacco, alcohol, and drugs, and take prudent steps to avoid accidents. The proverbial "apple a day keeps the doctor away" is not so far from the truth, after all.

Second, individuals should actively participate in their own medical care. They should schedule regular medical and dental checkups. Should they develop an illness or injury, they should know when to treat themselves and when to seek professional help. To gain the maximum benefit from any medical treatment that they do require, individuals must become partners in that treatment. For instance, they should understand the effects and side effects of medications. I counsel young physicians that there is no such thing as too much information when talking with patients. But the corollary is the patient must know enough about the nuts and bolts of the healing process to understand what the doctor is telling him. That is at least partially the patient's responsibility.

Education is equally necessary for us to understand the ethical and public policy issues in health care today. Sometimes individuals will encounter these issues in making decisions about their own treatment or that of family members. Other citizens may encounter them as jurors in medical malpractice cases. But we all become involved, indirectly, when we elect our public officials, from school board members to the president. Should surrogate parenting be legal? To what extent is drug testing desirable, legal, or necessary? Should there be public funding for family planning, hospitals, various types of medical research, and medical care for the indigent? How should we allocate scant technological resources, such as kidney dialysis and organ transplants? What is the proper role of government in protecting the rights of patients?

What are the broad goals of public health in the United States today? In 1980, the Public Health Service issued a report aptly entitled *Promoting Health-Preventing Disease: Objectives for the Nation.* This report expressed its goals in terms of mortality and in terms of intermediate goals in education and health improvement. It identified 15 major concerns: controlling high blood pressure; improving family planning; improving pregnancy care and infant health; increasing the rate of immunization; controlling sexually transmitted diseases; controlling the presence of toxic agents and radiation in the environment; improving occupational safety and health; preventing accidents; promoting water fluoridation and dental health; controlling infectious diseases; decreasing smoking; decreasing alcohol and drug abuse; improving nutrition; promoting physical fitness and exercise; and controlling stress and violent behavior.

For healthy adolescents and young adults (ages 15 to 24), the specific goal was a 20% reduction in deaths, with a special focus on motor vehicle injuries and alcohol and drug abuse. For adults (ages 25 to 64), the aim was 25% fewer deaths, with a concentration on heart attacks, strokes, and cancers.

Smoking is perhaps the best example of how individual behavior can have a direct impact on health. Today cigarette smoking is recognized as the most important single preventable cause of death in our society. It is responsible for more cancers and more cancer deaths than any other known agent; is a prime risk factor for heart and blood vessel disease, chronic bronchitis, and emphysema; and is a frequent cause of complications in pregnancies and of babies born prematurely, underweight, or with potentially fatal respiratory and cardiovascular problems.

Since the release of the Surgeon General's first report on smoking in 1964, the proportion of adult smokers has declined substantially, from 43% in 1965 to 30.5% in 1985. Since 1965, 37 million people have quit smoking. Although there is still much work to be done if we are to become a "smoke-free society," it is heartening to note that public health and public education efforts—such as warnings on cigarette packages and bans on broadcast advertising—have already had significant effects.

In 1835, Alexis de Tocqueville, a French visitor to America, wrote, "In America the passion for physical well-being is general." Today, as then, health and fitness are front-page items. But with the greater scientific and technological resources now available to us, we are in a far stronger position to make good health care available to everyone. And with the greater technological threats to us as we approach the 21st century, the need to do so is more urgent than ever before. Comprehensive information about basic biology, preventive medicine, medical and surgical treatments, and related ethical and public policy issues can help you arm yourself with the knowledge you need to be healthy throughout your life.

# FOREWORD

Solomon H. Snyder, M.D.

**M**ental disorders represent the number one health problem for the United States and probably for the entire human population. Some studies estimate that approximately one-third of all Americans suffer from some sort of emotional disturbance. Depression of varying severity will affect as many as 20 percent of all of us at one time or another in our lives. Severe anxiety is even more common.

Adolescence is a time of particular susceptibility to emotional problems. Teenagers are undergoing significant changes in their brain as well as their physical structure. The hormones that alter the organs of reproduction during puberty also influence the way we think and feel. At a purely psychological level, adolescents must cope with major upheavals in their lives. After years of not noticing the opposite sex, they find themselves romantically attracted but must painfully learn the skills of social interchange both for superficial, flirtatious relationships and for genuine intimacy. Teenagers must develop new ways of relating to their parents. Adolescents strive for independence. Yet, our society is structured in such a way that teenagers must remain dependent on their parents for many more years. During adolescence, young men and women examine their own intellectual bents and begin to plan the type of higher education and vocation they believe they will find most fulfilling.

Because of all these challenges, teenagers are more emotionally volatile than adults. Passages from extreme exuberance to dejection are common. The emotional distress of completely normal adolescence can be so severe that the same disability in an adult would be labeled as major mental illness. Although most teenagers somehow muddle through and emerge unscathed, a number of problems are more frequent among adolescents than among adults. Many psychological aberrations reflect severe disturbances, although these are sometimes not regarded as "psychiatric." Eating disorders, to which young adults are especially vulnerable, are an example. An

11

extremely large number of teenagers diet to great excess even though they are not overweight. Many of them suffer from a specific disturbance referred to as anorexia nervosa, a form of self-starvation that is just as real a disorder as diabetes. The same is true for those who eat compulsively and then sometimes force themselves to vomit. They may be afflicted with bulimia.

Depression is also surprisingly frequent among adolescents, although its symptoms may be less obvious in young people than they are in adults. And, because suicide occurs most frequently in those suffering from depression, we must be on the lookout for subtle hints of despondency in those close to us. This is especially urgent because teenage suicide is a rapidly worsening national problem.

The volumes on Psychological Disorders and Their Treatment in the ENCYCLOPEDIA OF HEALTH cover the major areas of mental illness, from mild to severe. They also emphasize the means available for getting help. *Anxiety and Phobias, Depression,* and *Schizophrenia* deal specifically with these forms of mental disturbance. *Child Abuse* and *Delinquency and Criminal Behavior* explore abnormalities of behavior that may stem from environmental and social influences as much as from biological or psychological illness. *Personality Disorders* and *Compulsive Behavior* explain how people develop disturbances of their overall personality. *Learning Disabilities* investigates disturbances of the mind that may reflect neurological derangements as much as psychological abnormalities. *Mental Retardation* explains the various causes of this many-sided handicap, including the genetic component, complications during pregnancy, and traumas during birth. *Suicide* discusses the epidemiology of this tragic phenomenon and outlines the assistance available to those who are at risk. *Stress Management* locates the sources of stress in contemporary society and considers formal strategies for coping with it. Finally, *Diagnosing and Treating Mental Illness* explains to the reader how professionals sift through various signs and symptoms to define the exact nature of the various mental disorders and fully describes the most effective means of alleviating them.

Fortunately, when it comes to psychological disorders, knowing the facts is a giant step toward solving the problems.

# THE BETRAYAL
# OF TRUST

**W**hen we think of children, we think of defenseless vulner-ability and the innocent joy that children often exhibit over the smallest of things. And then there is trust—the sacred trust between a child and his or her guardian, whether it be parent, relative, or some other authority figure. When this trust is be-trayed, the results are both tragic and painful. When an innocent, vulnerable child is brutalized by a person he or she may love or trust, child abuse occurs.

The topic of child abuse is not an easy one to talk about or read about. Children are regarded very highly in virtually every part of the world. A great deal of time, energy, and emotion goes into securing a happy childhood for our young ones, to keeping them safe and helping them develop into mature, balanced adults. Naturally, any violation of this unspoken pact is viewed with horror. Too often, the subject of child abuse is ignored or spoken of only in whispers.

But the difficulty of discussing child abuse does not compare with the pain an abused child may have been forced to endure. For this reason alone it is necessary to talk about the problem; to discover which people are more likely to become tormenters, discuss what behavior is considered abuse, and find out what programs and facilities are available to help an abused child.

Child abuse is not a rare disease; in 1987 approximately 2.3 million cases of child abuse and neglect were reported to authorities in the United States alone. Furthermore, most health professionals believe that nearly 1% of all American children are subjected to abuse or neglect each year. The U.S. National Center on Child Abuse and Neglect reports that 40% of those identified as being abused or neglected are under 5 years of age; many are infants.

The incidence of child abuse has increased dramatically over the last decade. The 2.3 million cases reported in 1987 represented a rise of about 30% over the number of cases reported in 1983 and a striking increase over the 400,000 cases reported in 1976. The National Committee for Prevention of Child Abuse contends that child abuse grew at a 14% annual rate until 1984 and continues to grow at a slower 9% pace since then. Some of this decrease is due, no doubt, to increased public awareness of the problem and stricter enforcement of reporting laws. Yet there is still a long way to go in the battle against child abuse.

This volume will discuss the nature of child abuse, exploring the history of the problem and then examining the legal and social implications in present-day abuse cases. We will also discuss the different programs available to help victims of abuse and the measures social and health professionals are taking to control and prevent child abuse in the future.

• • • •

# CHAPTER 1

· · · · · · · · · · · · · · · · ·

# DEFINING
# CHILD ABUSE

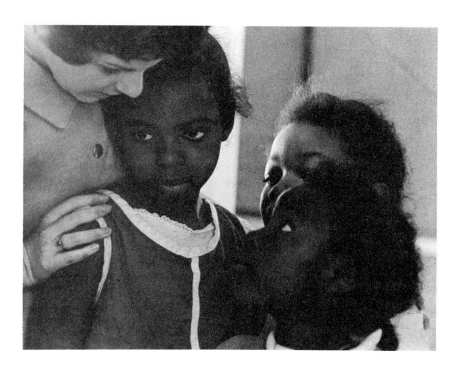

**A**lthough many people believe that child abuse occurs only when there is physical abuse, the crime actually includes several distinct types of mistreatment. In 1985 the Canadian Medical Association formulated a comprehensive definition of child abuse (the incidence of child abuse in Canada is almost equal to that of the United States). Their report stated, "Child abuse occurs if a person who has the care or custody of a child causes or allows the child to suffer any of the following: physical harm,

*Dr. Eli Newberger serves as director of a program to prevent and treat child abuse at the Children's Hospital Medical Center in Boston.*

such as external or internal bruises, burns, fractures, wounds, brain damage or poisoning; malnutrition (including dehydration) or mental ill-health of a degree that if not immediately remedied could seriously impair growth and development or result in permanent injury or death; or sexual molestation."

Breaking these elements down into categories, the phrase "child abuse and neglect" includes (1)physical abuse, (2)sexual abuse, (3)emotional abuse and child neglect, and (4)failure to thrive. It may be more useful and more accurate to think of these varieties of child abuse as a spectrum of mistreatment. Dr. Eli Newberger, pediatrician and director of a program to prevent and treat child abuse at the Children's Hospital Medical Center in Boston, suggested in an article in the *New England Journal of Medicine* that "failure to thrive, neglect, and abuse form a continuum of symptoms, perhaps from the same causes."

*Physical abuse* is what most people think of when they hear the term *child abuse*. Physical abuse may be deliberately shaking, hitting, or burning a child or in any other way inflicting deliberate physical injury. In most cases it is clear when an act is abusive. Cultural differences, however, may sometimes cloud the issue, as we will see in the next chapter.

Of the more than 2 million cases of child abuse and neglect reported in the United States each year, more than 200,000 comprise physical abuse. Out of every 1,000 babies born each year, it is estimated that 6 will be abused while still children. When physical abuse of infants and children does occur, it often causes severe injury. Dr. Katherine Christoffel, of Children's Hospital in Chicago, estimates that about 10% of injuries in children younger than 5 years of age that require treatment in hospital emergency rooms are the result of a violent act.

Although physical abuse is the smallest fraction of all abuse and neglect, it is the most lethal form of the crime. Physical abuse is the single greatest cause of death in infants between 6 and 12 months of age. Dr. Janine Jason of the Centers for Disease Control, in Atlanta, analyzed homicides involving children in 1979 and found that almost all murders of children younger than three years were committed by a parent or guardian.

Dr. Christoffel used data from the World Health Organization to estimate how many children die in other countries as a result of child abuse. She found that although fatal child abuse is a worldwide phenomenon, some countries have very low rates of childhood death from abuse. These countries include Denmark, Ireland, Italy, the Netherlands, Norway, and Sweden. In these countries deaths from abuse of babies under one year of age are virtually nonexistent.

There is indirect evidence that *severe* physical abuse (as opposed to child abuse in general, which is on the rise) may be decreasing, perhaps as a result of greater social awareness and more openly expressed societal disapproval. A survey sponsored by the National Institute of Mental Health compared the number of parents who admitted that they had physically abused their children in 1985 with the number of those reporting such violence in 1975. The fraction of parents reporting severe violence dropped from 14% in 1975 to 10.7% in 1985. If these numbers are accurate, it implies that thousands fewer children were the victims of extreme violence in 1985.

There is some question, however, about the reliability of this and other similar surveys. Some officials speculate that public pressure and fear of prosecution may lead some parents to respond untruthfully, playing down the frequency or severity of abuse.

*Sexual abuse,* or sexual molestation, includes all forms of sexual exploitation of a defenseless child by an older person. Sexual use of a young child by an adolescent may also be considered sexual abuse. Many degrees of sexual contact are covered by sexual abuse, including fondling a child's genitals, manual masturbation of the abuser by the child, masturbation by a male abuser against any part of the child's body, all forms of oral-genital contact between a child and an adult, exhibitionism of an adult in front of a child, and vaginal or anal intercourse with a child. Penetration, either attempted or completed, is not necessary for sexual abuse to be present and occurs in only a minority of instances.

Sexual abuse or misuse of children, particularly girls, is relatively frequent. Sexual abuse constitutes perhaps 10% of all reports of child abuse and neglect registered each year with the National Center on Child Abuse and Neglect. But most professionals working in this area believe that this is a low estimate, because many incidents of sexual abuse go unreported and undetected. According to Dr. Gloria Bachmann, a gynecologist at the University of Medicine and Dentistry of New Jersey, as many as 500,000 cases of child sexual abuse actually occur each year. As a result, between 1 in 4 and 1 in 3 of all women has had a forced sexual experience with an adult before she has reached the age of 18.

Boys also suffer sexual abuse, although not as frequently as girls. The University of Michigan's educational videotape "Sexually Misused Children" states that approximately one-third of abused children are males, and between 10% and 12% of males reaching the age of 18 have been abused. When boys are sexually abused, they are more often subjected to violent treatment.

Sexual abuse is also found in other countries. Statistics from Great Britain suggest that the problem of child sexual abuse has been growing rapidly there. The British government estimates that 1,500 children suffered sexual abuse or sexual molestation in 1984; by 1986 this figure had risen sharply to 6,000 sexually molested or abused children.

*Emotional abuse* and *child neglect* make up the large majority of all cases of child abuse and neglect reported to state and national authorities each year. In emotional abuse cases children are not physically assaulted, but they may be continually called names, shouted at, and verbally abused. A physical counterpart to emotional abuse is neglect, which may take the form of regularly leaving a child alone without adequate care or in dangerous circumstances, or not providing adequate nutrition for a child.

*Failure to thrive* is a particular form of neglect seen in young infants. The child simply does not grow, acts listless, and appears sickly. Children who suffer this form of neglect are among the smallest one-third of children of their age and fail to develop appropriate mental and emotional skills, although they do not have a detectable illness to account for the slow growth.

Doctors now think that failure to thrive may be a result of a lack of emotional nurturing from the infant's mother more than a lack of nutritional support. Lack of maternal nurturing may be due to the mother's inability to satisfy the child's emotional needs, failure to form a mother-infant bond soon after birth, or to some combination of these elements. In some cases these children increase their growth rate rapidly when they are separated from their parents and put with caring foster parents.

## Recognizing the Symptoms

As one might expect, being abused can have a serious detrimental impact on a child. A number of changes, either psychological or physical, are usually evident and can prove valuable in recognizing a case of abuse.

*Many so-called missing children are actually runaways; often they are escaping homes in which they were abused.*

Immediate behavioral changes are often evident in abused children. In fact, certain specific changes are cited as tip-offs that abuse has occurred and as ways of corroborating a youngster's report of abuse. For instance, a physician examining a very young child who has suffered abuse may observe an inappropriate emotional response. Such a child may either be abnormally passive in the face of a painful examination or medical procedure or intensely apprehensive of unthreatening procedures. A youngster may also express fear of his or her parents or express a desire to stay in the hospital rather than go home.

Other possible signals that a child is emotionally troubled by abuse are serious sleep disturbances, regression to infant actions (such as wetting the bed or clinging), sudden difficulty in school, or depression.

So-called missing children are often another consequence of child abuse and neglect. Popular wisdom has it that most such children are abducted by malicious strangers. That is not true. Many are taken by a divorced parent locked in a bitter custodial divorce battle. But the National Center for Missing and Exploited Children estimates that 95% of missing children are really runaways; many runaways are victims of child abuse and neglect.

Diana Griego is a Denver newspaper reporter who won a 1986 Pulitzer Prize for a series of articles on missing children. "We have to wonder," Ms. Griego wrote, "about the life from which those children are trying to escape. Do they feel driven by neglect and a lack of time to look elsewhere for love?"

The vast majority of the information about the frequency and effects of the various forms of child abuse that we have discussed so far has been obtained in the past generation. For most of the history of humankind, there has been very little discussion of the problem of child abuse. That was not because such actions did not exist. As we shall see in Chapter 2, mistreating children in one form or another has persisted for as long as recorded history.

•    •    •    •

# CHAPTER 2
· · · · · · · · · · · · · · · ·
# HISTORICAL AND CULTURAL PERSPECTIVES

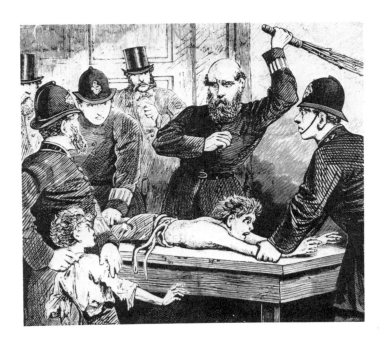

Child abuse is not unique to the United States, to Western culture, or to modern times. In fact, violence against infants and children is at least as old as recorded history. Concepts of childhood have ranged from that of the innocent in Greek art to that of the child as a miniature adult during the Middle Ages in Europe. Treatment of children by and large has reflected the society's view of the nature of the child. During medieval times, for instance, there was neither a definition of childhood nor a vocabulary to differentiate it from adulthood. Treatment of children during this period was accordingly based on the perception of children as adults in need of training, leading to generally rigid and brutal treatment of children.

The core of society's attitude toward children has traditionally consisted of two beliefs: one, that children are their parents' responsibility and, two, that parents own their children. These two beliefs can be somewhat contradictory. A child's fate has always depended on whether a society or an individual family has placed more emphasis on the former part of this pair of attitudes or the latter.

Infanticide (the killing of infants) was practiced in such ancient civilizations as China and classical Greece, especially the city-state of Sparta. This practice may have been a way of coping with the tenuous state of survival and the scarcity of food and resources that has persisted for the vast majority of the human population throughout history. In the Bible the stories of Isaac and Moses show us that the killing of infants was part of Hebrew social custom. And early Roman law gave the father the absolute right of life or death over his children.

The Sacrifice of Isaac, *by the Italian painter Caravaggio, shows an angel stopping Abraham from killing his son. Many biblical stories reflect the ancient belief that the father has the absolute right of life or death over his children.*

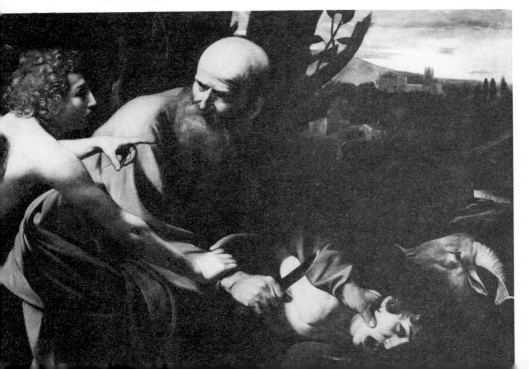

*This baby was put in a fruit basket and deserted by his mother in 1936. During the 1950s the U.S. government established a number of social welfare agencies designed specifically for the interests of abandoned and abused children.*

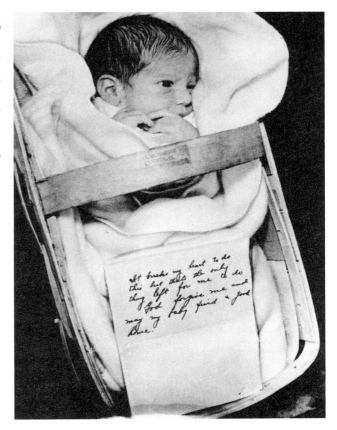

When the Christian religion gained sway in the Western world, it used its influence to counteract infanticide. In the 4th century the Roman state yielded to this influence and made infanticide a capital offense. Such laws marked the adoption of the revolutionary principle that the state can intervene in the family on behalf of the child.

Still, the killing of babies, especially illegitimate ones, continued through the 19th century. Abandonment was as often the means of getting rid of unwanted children as was outright murder. During medieval times infants were killed, and punishment for older children was strict and frequently brutal—often, ironically, in the name of religion. The objective of these rigorous disciplinary practices was to teach children to behave in a righteous way. Followers of Protestant religious reformer John Calvin

*The 18th-century French philosopher Jean-Jacques Rousseau was a pioneer of the belief that children who are physically abused are more likely to become abusers themselves.*

believed that misbehaving children should be flogged to eliminate their innate depravity; this was a common practice through the 17th century.

Attitudes toward humankind and particularly toward children changed during the 18th century. Many perceived childhood as an idyllic time and children as noble and innocent. Evil was perceived as something that arose in a person's soul as a result of ill treatment by adults in society. Therefore, philosophers of this period, such as Jean-Jacques Rousseau, believed that routine corporal punishment and physical abuse were more likely to lead to mean-spirited, rather than benevolent, adults.

Nevertheless, incidents of child abuse remained. In fact, the mistreatment of children reached astonishing heights in England during the period from about the mid-18th century to the mid-19th. During this period, known as the Industrial Revolution, machine manufacturing became an alternative to manual work. Sweatshop and factory owners took advantage of the absence of laws preventing children from working and created a large child-labor force, with extremely low wages and inhumane working conditions. Many parents felt that children were their property and, consequently, sold them as cheap labor.

In some cases children 5 and 6 years of age were forced to work from 13 to 16 hours a day. Owners of cotton mills collected orphans and children of poor parents to work in the factories for some scraps of food and a place to drop at the end of the grueling workday. Many children were injured or crippled working in mines.

The push for reforming working conditions and child-labor laws in England began as early as 1802 but met resistance from political and religious leaders. Finally, in 1878, legislation was passed making the minimum age of employees 10 years, restricting the work of children between the ages of 10 and 14 to alternate days, and limiting work by older children to 12 hours with a break of 2 hours for meals and rest.

The earliest legislative measures against child abuse in the United States were reforms directed against the widespread use of child labor. For instance, in Massachusetts in 1836, the legislature passed a law prohibiting the employment of any child under 15 years of age who had received less than 3 months of

*Before the creation of child labor laws, children were used as a cheap source of labor. Even young children, such as the oyster shuckers shown here, were forced to work 13 to 16 hours a day.*

schooling in the previous year. During the next 2 decades, many states established a minimum age, usually 12 years, for child laborers in textile mills. Protection of children from outright abuse was carried one step further in the United States in 1875 with the founding of the American Society for the Prevention of Cruelty to Children. The founder of this group was a New Yorker named Henry Bergh, who had founded the American Society for the Prevention of Cruelty to Animals in 1866. It is ironic that for almost 10 years the United States had an organization to protect dogs and cats but none to protect children.

In 1912 the U.S. government established the Children's Bureau as a federal agency to oversee the health and welfare of children. During the last 30 years county social welfare agencies that represent the interests of children have been established. Such agencies are affiliated under the Denver-based American Humane Association as the American Association for Protecting Children.

During the 1970s the number of agencies designed to promote the welfare of children expanded. This followed the exposure of the controversial topic of child abuse in 1961–62 by Dr. C. Henry Kempe, a pediatrician at the University of Colorado Medical Center in Denver.

Before Dr. Kempe's work publicized it, child abuse was not nationally recognized as a major problem. Writing in the *Journal of the American Medical Association* in 1984, Dr. Marilyn Heins describes the situation before Dr. Kempe's work: "With the onset of better economic conditions in our country, children became better cared for. They were clean and well fed; parents had more leisure time to devote to their children. The American childhood seemed idyllic when compared with earlier times and with childhood in other nations. This likely led to a mind-set that held that parental abuse of children was not possible."

Tragically, however, such abuse *was* going on. It was discovered by physicians, particularly radiologists, who saw multiple traumatic fractures of children's arms and legs, for several years. Dr. Frederic Silverman, a radiologist, believed in the reality of deliberate child injury. He wrote in 1953, "Caretakers may permit trauma and be unaware of it, may recognize trauma but forget or be reluctant to admit it, or may deliberately injure the child and deny it." This statement, while seeming quite tame by today's standards, was actually quite radical for the time.

Nonetheless, the problem was not seen as common, according to Dr. Heins: "Although we can only speculate on how widely these articles were read, it is clear that child abuse was considered a minor aberration of parenting that rarely was seen and that was likely to be found in children of disadvantaged families."

In this atmosphere Dr. Kempe began to evaluate the problem of child abuse in earnest. He found that 10% of emergency-room visits for trauma in children at the University of Colorado Medical Center were due to child abuse and that many of these incidents occurred in middle-class families. The topic was just waiting for someone to bring it out into the open. Dr. Kempe finally arranged a session on child abuse at the 1961 meeting of the American Academy of Pediatrics.

As it turned out, many doctors had been seeing cases of child abuse, but none had been courageous enough to take up the struggle themselves. They denied the problem, probably in large part because they did not know what to do next. Once Dr. Kempe brought it out into the open in a respectable medical forum, however, doctors could admit what they had been seeing.

The public also began paying considerable attention to child abuse at that time. This was partly because of the emotional nature of the problem, but it was also due to Dr. Kempe's coining a catchy name—"battered-child syndrome"—as well as the publication of his observations on child abuse in the widely read *Journal of the American Medical Association* in 1962. Child abuse quickly became a topic on television shows, including "Ben Casey" and "Dr. Kildare," as well as in popular magazines such as *Life* and *Good Housekeeping*.

All of this work and publicity led to the founding in 1972 of the C. Henry Kempe National Center for the Prevention and Treatment of Child Abuse and Neglect as part of the University of Colorado Medical Center in Denver. This is a hands-on center providing treatment as well as resources for the education of professionals.

In 1974 Congress passed the Federal Child Abuse Prevention and Treatment Act (the Schroeder-Mondale Act), which established the National Center on Child Abuse and Neglect in Washington, D.C., to sponsor and fund research and demonstration projects and to furnish information. Many other organizations have since arisen.

## Cultural Differences

In addition to a historical perspective on child abuse, it is helpful to have some appreciation of how differences in culture can affect the interpretation of this concept. We have already spoken of infanticide. Even in the 20th century this practice continues in some countries, primarily as a means of destroying defective offspring and to control population growth. In modern-day China, where parents have been restricted to having only one child as a means of controlling population and avoiding over-crowding, the killing of baby girls is considered almost a form of birth control because male children are traditionally favored.

Traditional folk remedies are cited by Dr. Newberger in an article in the *New England Journal of Medicine* as examples of practices that are socially permitted in another country even though they would be considered child abuse in the United States:

> In Vietnam, a four-year-old child was forced to submit to the practice of Cao Gio, or coin-rubbing, in which a child's oiled back is stroked with a coin until bruises appear, to help rid the body of 'bad winds.' It is unclear how painful or harmful this is to the child. . . . In Latin America, a folk remedy for depression of the soft spot on an infant's head prescribes holding the infant by the ankles while dipping the crown of his head into very hot water. This practice may cause both scalded skin and hemorrhage around the brain.

In the next chapter, we will discuss sexual abuse of children—a topic that has come to light only in recent years in the United States and that is still in great need of explanation and investigation.

• • • •

# CHAPTER 3

. . . . . . . . . . . . .

# CHILD SEXUAL ABUSE

When I encountered my first case of child abuse in 1972, there was no public interest or concern about sexual victimization of children. That year, I saw a six-year-old boy who was brought to a VD clinic by his mother because he had painful pus-like discharge from his penis. The little boy had a gonorrhea infection of his urethra. We later learned that he had acquired it because he had been sexually abused by a 14-year-old boy. Nothing I had learned in medical school or in an internal medicine residency had prepared me in any way to deal medically or socially with him or with his problem. I was shocked, confused, more than a little intimidated and desperately looking for guidelines and answers.

*—Dr. Suzanne M. Sgroi, executive director of a private treatment center for child sexual abuse in Connecticut, speaking at the 1986 meeting of the American College of Obstetrics and Gynecology.*

Although physical abuse was brought out of the closet in the early 1960s, sexual abuse has only been discussed openly within the last 10 years in our society. Abuse involving sex and sexuality brings such intense emotional trauma to the victim and causes greater emotional distress to those of us hearing of it than physical abuse does. Unfortunately, this makes it more difficult for the abused person to report the incident, especially if the victim is a young child.

Psychologist James Kent, Ph.D., of the Children's Evaluation Center in Los Angeles, distinguishes the different psychological bases of the two types of abuse. Physical abuse serves as an emotional outlet for an angry, frustrated adult with poor impulse control. But in sexual abuse, he says, sexual gratification, coupled with poor impulse control, is the precipitating combination.

It is necessary to address sexual abuse of children separately because several myths have grown up around child sexual abuse. It is important to dispel these myths in order to have a clear picture of the problem. Without an accurate perception of child sexual abuse it is unlikely that effective steps can be taken to control it. The following are some common myths that people have about child sexual abuse.

*Myth #1: Sexual abuse of children is committed by strangers.* We have a social myth that child abuse is committed by mentally ill persons with sadistic, twisted minds; people who are strangers to us and to our children.

According to a 1985 report on child abuse by the Canadian Medical Association, however, this is not usually the case. Indeed, the report states that "most commonly, the sexual abuser seems normal in general appearance and behavior and in most cases is known to the victim. It is uncommon for the abuser to be psychotic, sexually perverted or deranged."

In fact, most sexual abuse of children—up to 90%, some experts estimate—is committed by someone the child knows. Several very recent cases support this statistic.

- In Georgia, in 1987, the highly respected founder and former director of a psychiatric treatment center for adolescent boys pleaded guilty to numerous counts of sodomy with former patients.
- In 1988 it was revealed that a Roman Catholic priest in Seattle, Washington, had a 20-year history of sexually molesting children.
- In 1988 in Newark, New Jersey, a female teacher was convicted of sexually assaulting 19 children at a day-care center.

In 1988 Dr. Gloria Bachmann of the University of Medicine and Dentistry of New Jersey reported typical findings concerning sexual abuse of children. Dr. Bachmann related that male family members are the most likely sexual abusers of children under age 11. Seven times as many stepfathers as biological fathers are reported as sexual abusers (which may only mean that biological fathers are less likely to be detected or reported). Grandfathers, uncles, and older brothers have also been known to commit sexual abuse.

This, perhaps, is one of the most important myths to be dispelled. For if society refuses to believe that family members—good family men, wonderful mothers, adoring uncles—are capable of sexually abusing a child, then victims will be afraid to come forward and ask for help. Or, if they do, they will not be believed.

*Myth #2: Sexual abuse of children typically involves violence and rape.* Dr. Sgroi, director of the Saint Joseph College Institute for the Treatment and Control of Child Sexual Abuse in West Hartford, Connecticut, found that fewer than 20% of a group of child sexual abusers whom she studied used force. Most of the abusers tricked the child into the sexual activity by presenting it as a game or by offering the child a reward. "We need to remember," she says, "that we teach children to do what adults tell them to do. Most children cooperate with their abusers—they do what they are told."

*A young girl enjoys a ride on a swing. Children often trust those who abuse them, believing their abuser when he or she says that molestation is actually just another game or pleasurable activity.*

Dr. Kent has found that sexual molesters of children are persuasive more often than coercive. "Most pedophiles [child molesters] are lovers of children," he says. "They are very seductive toward children and children are attracted to them."

*Myth #3: Sexual abuse of children is usually carried out by a "dirty old man."* Abusers are typically middle-class persons of respectable appearance, with a median age of 35, according to Dr. Bachmann.

*Myth #4: Sexual abuse of children is not damaging.* Even if the victim is not physically harmed, sexual abuse can be traumatic because it essentially forces a youngster to do something that he or she does not understand and to which he or she cannot give true consent. The victims may wonder what they did to deserve this treatment. They begin to feel strange and different from other people their own age, and their guilt and shame may make them withdraw from companionship with peers, resulting in isolation and loneliness.

Some sexual abusers argue that the child enjoyed the sexual activity, and so there was nothing wrong with it. Dr. Kent disputes that notion. "When the offender says, 'She likes it,' that's somewhat true," he acknowledges. "After a certain age we all have the capacity to enjoy sex. But it is still harmful to the child because he or she is not in a position to give consent."

Serious emotional damage from sexual abuse is compounded because, for the helpless dependent child, there is no escape from the assault. To try to cope, the child may adopt abnormal roles and behaviors, such as acting precociously seductive or prom-

*Children who are victims of sexual abuse often feel isolated and alone.*

iscuous. Most important, a sexual abuser puts a child in a situation that denies him or her a normal sequence of development. The incestuous father, for example, robs his daughter of the relationship to a parent that is advisable for healthy growing up.

## The Sexual Abuser

So far we have focused to a great extent on myths and taboos about child sexual abuse. We have seen that children are often molested or abused by a seemingly wholesome, otherwise normal person, who is typically a relative or acquaintance, and only very rarely by a person who has an overt mental illness. But that realization raises a very puzzling question: If sexual abusers of children are so much like other people, why do they commit this offense? What makes the difference between an ordinary, otherwise normal father who sexually molests his baby daughter

A father and his young daughter enjoy the closeness of a warm, healthy father-daughter relationship. Tragically, some parents violate this natural intimacy by subjecting their children to sexual abuse.

and the vast majority of other fathers who do not take sexual liberties with their children?

Although it is never possible to explain completely such a fundamental deviation from normal behavior in apparently healthy people, experts in this field have identified several characteristics of sexual abusers that at least partly explain their actions. We have already mentioned that sexual abusers lack adequate impulse control when they feel sexual urges. Combined with a lack of self-control are other characteristics, according to the University of Michigan instructional videotape "Sexually Misused Children." A sexual abuser is often a domineering father or stepfather, one who has low self-esteem and makes up for it by bullying his children. According to the videotape, poor self-control can be further weakened by alcohol or substance abuse, and if the mother, who is often a female child's primary form of protection, is not available, either by absence, illness, or lack of assertive maternal caring.

Some of these factors were illustrated in a 1980 study of 73 cases of child sexual abuse done by Larry N. Scherzer, M.D., and Padma Lala, M.D., of the Johns Hopkins University School of Medicine. They verified other investigators' findings that the assailant was known to the victim in about 80% of instances. In addition, they reported that

- The mother was absent from the home in most cases.
- Half the time the assailant was identified as being drunk.

Drs. Scherzer and Lala also recognized social and personal stresses on the families in which sexual abuse took place that would tend to reduce further the self-respect of the abuser and to weaken personal and social restraint. "The families that we have observed are under continuing stress because of unemployment, low income, isolation from community resources and a non-intact family structure."

Some of the characteristics of child abuse we have described were present in a notorious instance that only came to light very recently. In 1988 Cheryl Crane, the daughter of movie actress and sex symbol Lana Turner, wrote her autobiography, *Detour: A Hollywood Story*. In her autobiography Ms. Crane reveals that for several years she suffered repeated episodes of sexual abuse from her stepfather, Lex Barker, the handsome actor who played Tarzan in the movies after Johnny Weismuller. Cheryl became increasingly disturbed, finally running away from home. When Ms. Turner found out what was going on, she split up with Barker, but Cheryl never did get the emotional support from her mother and the counseling that is necessary for healing in such cases.

This incident illustrates several elements often present in cases of childhood sexual abuse:

- A mother who is insecure about her husband or boyfriend.
- A mother who is also abused.
- A man who is apparently masculine and emotionally healthy but who has low self-esteem and poor impulse control.

Several of these same characteristics were found in the 1986 case of Cheryl Pierson, the Long Island teenager who arranged for someone to kill her father. Both her parents were infantile in their emotional development and turned to their daughter for needed fulfillment. Cheryl took over running the house when she was nine years old because her mother was seriously ill. In a common pattern, her father later turned to her as a surrogate wife as well.

In addition, Cheryl Pierson's mother knew about her husband's actions but did nothing to intervene, according to court testimony from Ms. Pierson's uncle. Cheryl's father was outwardly normal, and no indications of his sexual obsession with his daughter were seen by fellow workers or most of his relatives. In fact, his mother and sister testified that he was innocent and the daughter was lying. In Ms. Pierson's case, however, she was ultimately believed and is currently only under probation.

It is common to hear charges that a girl is lying when she says she has been sexually abused by her father or her mother's boyfriend. However, false reports of child sexual abuse are not common, and when they occur, they are usually found in the context of child custody cases and are initiated by one of the parents rather than by the child.

*Long Island teenager Cheryl Pierson served a prison sentence in 1987 for arranging to have her father killed after he made sexual advances to her younger sister. Mr. Pierson had allegedly sexually abused Cheryl for a number of years.*

According to a University of Michigan instructional videotape on child sexual abuse: "Children do not make up stories of sexual abuse. Small children need experience to describe sexual acts in detail. Stories of this nature are not childhood fantasies."

## Child Pornography

Child pornography is a form of sexual exploitation of children that involves more than private activity between two persons. Sex rings that produce magazines or videotapes of children engaging in sexual activity have a profoundly damaging effect on the children. Dr. Ann Wolbert Burgess of the University of Pennsylvania School of Nursing directed a study of 66 children who had been involved in sex rings between 1978 and 1981. She and her colleagues reported in the *American Journal of Psychiatry* that 75% of them had difficulty overcoming the experience. They suffered an emotional disorder similar to that found in Vietnam War veterans, called posttraumatic stress disorder. These children experienced painful recollections of the traumatic incidents, nightmares, hyperactivity, and difficulty sleeping.

What is striking about these sex rings—apart from the distressing fact that they exist—is that the child usually knows the offender. According to Dr. Burgess's study, the people who introduced the children into the pornographic activities were not strangers but trusted caretakers. Ringleaders included a grandfather, a teacher, a Scout leader, a sports coach, a school-bus driver, and the manager of the apartment building where one child lived. This familiarity would have to exist for repeated activity to continue over the course of weeks to months without outright kidnapping. The next chapter will examine abusers more closely. We will learn what type of person is most likely to abuse his or her child and what events or situations precipitate or instigate incidents of abuse.

## Treating the Problem

Sexual abuse is a public health problem of great magnitude, and we cannot combat it effectively if we persist in clinging to myths about who does it. Sexual abuse of children happens each day, melding into the normal fabric of our everyday society. It is not a rarity, and we must respond to it with more than outrage.

•     •     •     •

# CHAPTER 4

. . . . . . . . . . . . . . . . .

# BANISHING ILLUSIONS

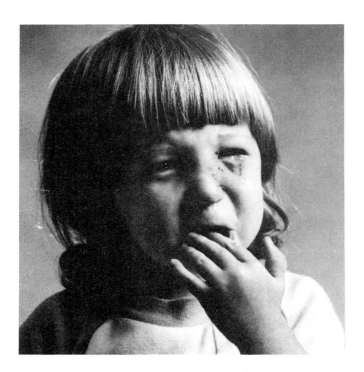

**A**s we noted in Chapter 3, myths about sexual abusers impede our willingness to accept accusations of abuse against persons who do not fit our stereotypes of an abuser. Myths about what abusers are like also make it harder to set up effective prevention and treatment programs. Those reasons apply to physical abuse as well as sexual abuse.

The best way to begin a discussion on who commits physical child abuse and why is to eliminate some misconceptions at the

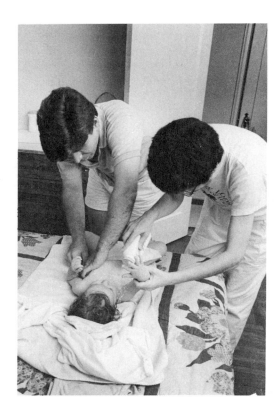

*A new mother whose husband not only offers emotional support but also shares in the care of the child is less likely to abuse her child.*

outset. All persons who work in this field agree that mental or emotional illness is not a major factor in physical child abuse. Richard D. Krugman, M.D., is director of the Kempe Center in Denver. He says, "In our experience, significantly less than 2 percent of abuse cases we deal with are inflicted by psychotics." When a psychosis is involved, Dr. Krugman added, it is often schizophrenia with paranoid ideas that include the child; for instance, a conviction that the devil sent the child.

A more concrete and detailed depiction of the differences between parents who abuse their children and those who do not is provided by an essay that appeared in the *New York Times* in May 1988. It was written by Judith Ungar, a career woman with two children. She recalls one time when her children were three years and six months old, and she was also taking care of two of a friend's children of the same ages:

I am three for four in naps. One of the babies—dry, fed, lullabied—continues to cry. And cry. I want to squeeze him quiet, not with the express intent of harming him but just to make him stop crying.

Why didn't I? Because my parents never hurt me? Because I never saw a child abused? Because I knew it was wrong? Because I could not bear to hurt a helpless baby? Because I feared the consequences? Probably all of the above.

I am blessed with healthy children, a loving and helpful husband, supportive family, friends, comfortable means and enough time away from the kids for other pursuits or for just being away from them.

So, how does someone with no husband (or the wrong one), with more children than means to feed and clothe them, living in substandard housing, with no competent sitters to relieve her, no extended family to help—how does that mother cope when the baby cries and cries?

As we are now painfully aware, the answer is that sometimes she doesn't. A woman who puts her 2-month-old son "under the water until he stopped crying" is not a different species of animal than I. Personal virtue is not the main thing that separates us.

Ms. Ungar's anecdote and her reflections provide us with several clues to how physical abuse of children comes about. Her impulse to harm a baby occurred in response to an inconsolably crying child. But she identified her childhood experiences, her current familial situation, and her social and economic circumstances as major factors in helping her to resist that impulse.

Writing in the June 22, 1984, issue of the *Journal of the American Medical Association*, Dr. Marilyn Heins of the University of Arizona College of Medicine in Tucson, grouped the factors precipitating child abuse into four categories:

1. A parent with the potential for abuse. Such parents were usually products of unhappy childhoods, often were themselves victims of abuse, are isolated, do not trust others, and have unrealistic expectations of children.

2. A child who usually exhibits some behavior that elicits a strong correction reaction from the parent, typically crying in an infant or talking back or disobedience in an older child.

3. A stressful situation or incident that serves as a trigger. This could be economic, such as loss of a job, or social, such as isolation from community support.

4. A culture in which corporal punishment is allowed or encouraged.

"In one sense, all parents have the potential to abuse," Dr. Heins wrote. "But most of us keep our murderous capabilities in check because we have impulse control, inner resources, and support systems." The abuser is lacking one or more of these.

We will consider, separately, each of the elements that contribute to child abuse.

## THE PERSONALITY OF THE ABUSER

James Kent, Ph.D., is a psychologist with the Children's Evaluation Center in Los Angeles. Several years ago he and a number of co-workers studied a group of persons who had physically abused children. Although Dr. Kent and his colleagues did not find a large number of thought or affect disorders among the abusers, they did find clearly identifiable personality problems. They grouped these problems into five categories:

1. Parents who routinely administered unusually harsh physical discipline. In these families both parents were very strict and they treated all children in this manner. These parents were the most likely to be arrested, because they admitted what they did. When confronted with the abused child they might say, "He talked back to me and I hit him." They did not lie because they believed that they were doing the right thing for the child. In these families the children "tended to turn out fairly well," according to Dr. Kent, probably because the abuse was not combined with rejection.

2. Abuse committed by the mother's boyfriend. Typically these were single-parent families, and often the youngster had behavioral problems after living alone with the mother. In many

cases the mother was also abused by the boyfriend. "Boyfriend abuse" can be lethal, Dr. Kent says. In some of these cases the baby is killed and buried in the backyard. On the other hand, if the child is removed from the abusive situation, he or she responds well to therapy.

It is important to recognize the role of the mother in allowing or even condoning physical abuse by her boyfriend. The attitude of the child's mother was illustrated in a 1988 Atlanta, Georgia, case, in which a 27-year-old man beat a boy to death in what the judge called an instance of "runaway discipline." The harsh physical punishment started when the boy wet his pants, and it escalated until death occurred. According to the newspaper account, both the mother of the dead boy and the man's ex-wife testified on the boyfriend's behalf: "The conviction came despite emotionally charged testimony by [the killer's] ex-wife and by his fiancee that he had a fatherly relationship with the boy and spent many hours playing with him and teaching him to spell while his mother was at work."

*Stressful situations within the family sometimes lead to abuse. In this 1948 photo a woman offers her four children for sale, an illegal practice today. The woman's husband had lost his job, and they were facing eviction.*

*Child abuse is not necessarily physical maltreatment. As this poster from the National Committee for the Prevention of Child Abuse suggests, a child can be hurt just as cruelly by emotional abuse.*

3. Parents who come from depressed and abused backgrounds and raise their children the same way, because that is the only way they know. There are four times as many incidents of child abuse among people who were abused as children. "These parents do not have a good inventory of childhood experiences," Dr. Kent says. Abuse by people who were abused as children makes up about 40 percent of physical abuse of children.

4. Families in which there is an unstable father who is unemployed or underemployed. Often the mother works to support the family, which further undermines many men's self-esteem. To aggravate the father's loss of face, the older children may challenge him. He responds with physical force.

5. Situations involving role reversal. A parent, often a single mother, may expect something of the child, some desired response to bolster the mother's self-image. If the child does not respond as wished, the mother feels inadequate, a failure. She often turns this guilt and anger on the child.

## CRYING BABIES

Ms. Ungar was not alone in finding that a crying baby triggers thoughts of physical abuse. That seems to be a very common stimulus to battering—often lethal—of infants.

Psychologist Ann Frodi of the University of Rochester studied this matter in some detail and published her findings in a 1981 article in the *American Journal of Mental Efficiency*. She concluded:

> There is a substantial amount of anecdotal evidence suggesting that infant crying often serves as a final spark triggering an abusive mother; a majority of women mentioned "incessant crying," "grating sound of the cry," or "whining for prolonged periods of time" as factors precipitating the abuse event.

In one study conducted in 1968 by J. Weston and cited by Dr. Frodi, excessive crying was given as the reason for battering by 80 percent of parents who abused infants less than 1 year old. Infants at risk for abuse, such as those who are premature or sickly, seem to have more irritating cries. "These cries are said to be so unpleasant that they override differences in maternal style," Dr. Frodi found.

It is not unreasonable to assume that a man who is not a baby's father would be less tolerant of that baby's crying than if he had been the biologic father.

## STRESSED FAMILIES

When a child with behavioral problems is in the same family with a parent who is not psychologically able to provide benevolent care, the stage is set for physical abuse. But in most cases, particularly with older children, additional factors are needed to precipitate the abuse. These are usually provided by stress, arising either within the family or from the family's interaction with society.

One simple and common type of stress arising within the family structure is the birth of twins. The association between twins and physical abuse was demonstrated in a study reported in *Pediatrics* in 1982 by Jessie R. Groothuis, M.D., and his co-workers of the Medical College of Ohio and Nashville General Hospital. They found that 2.4% of families without twins were reported for maltreatment, compared to a much higher 18.7% of families with twins. "Large families and inadequate spacing of children increase the risk for abuse," Dr. Groothuis and his colleagues concluded.

Dr. Janine Jason, of the Centers for Disease Control (CDC), looked for factors that increased the risk of physical abuse. In addition to verifying that abuse is more common in large families, she found abuse more frequent in families lacking either a biological mother or a biological father and in families needing public assistance. Absence of one or both biological parents is an especially strong indicator of possible child abuse. Half of all abused children are stepchildren, who are abused four to five times more often than natural children. In addition, Dr. Jason reported, young adolescent parents are more prone to commit abuse. Clearly these are all factors that either increase the degree of stress on a family or reduce the ability of the parent(s) to cope with stress.

Perhaps unsurprisingly, another factor determining if a child is likely to be abused is whether the parents wanted to have the child to begin with. William A. Altemeier III, M.D., and his colleagues at Vanderbilt University Hospital in Nashville, Tennessee, interviewed 1,400 low-income mothers in a prenatal clinic. They then tracked the mothers for two years. Twenty-three of the women were reported for child abuse during that time.

When the doctors looked back at the interviews conducted during pregnancy to see whether the abusive mothers had answered any questions differently from the nonabusive mothers, they found three differences. One related to the personality of the mothers: Abusive mothers reported more aggressive feelings and acts. The second concerned the women's childhood: Abusive mothers more often said that their childhood had been lacking in emotional support from their parents. The third factor was

*Women with close families can often rely upon their emotional support when raising their children.*

associated with the pregnancy: "Significantly more [mothers in the abuse category] were carrying an unplanned and unwanted pregnancy and described an adverse emotional status associated with their condition," Dr. Altemeier and his colleagues wrote. The investigators also found that the women's feelings about the pregnancy were not disguised or subtle: "Rejection of the pregnancy was overt and on a conscious level."

Of course, many babies who are unwanted are the result of teenage pregnancies. The birthrate among teenage single women continues to be much higher in the United States than in any other industrialized country, according to a 1987 report from the U.S. Centers for Disease Control. In 1983, the last year for which accurate figures are available, 87 out of every 1,000 American women between 15 and 19 years of age gave birth. In most cases the woman and the child's father do not form a stable relationship, and the young, inexperienced mother is left on her own to care for a child without any help and without a job.

Closely related to the statistics on the birthrate among unmarried women are those concerning U.S. households that are headed by single women. According to the Bureau of Labor Statistics, almost 26 percent of white households and 44 percent of black households were headed by a single woman in 1986. The stresses on the single mother—both from the unrelieved demands of caring for one or more infants and from anxieties about her future—can be enough to drive her to extreme measures. Child abuse or neglect is often the result.

Another interesting fact put forward by Dr. Newberger is that doctors and social workers are less likely to report a white middle-class man or woman as an abuser.

Dr. Newberger gathered supporting evidence for this assertion in a study of abusers that he and sociologist Robert L. Hampton, Ph.D., published in the *American Journal of Public Health* in 1985. They found that doctors in hospitals only reported half of the cases of abuse that they encountered and that the cases not reported were not randomly chosen. These factors distinguished unreported cases: The mother was more apt to be white, the family income was likely to be higher than in reported cases, and the mother was more often the suspected abuser.

*An Eskimo woman poses with her family. It was once believed that child abuse only occurred in poor families. Today, however, most people have come to realize that poor people are not as a rule abusive.*

In addition to being unjust and dangerous, this bias has a more subtle, but no less damaging, effect. "In selectively ignoring the prevalence of child abuse in more affluent, majority homes," Dr. Newberger and Dr. Hampton wrote, "we may be perpetuating a myth that child abusers are 'out there,' and that homes like ours are free of violence." Just as with sexual abuse, that bias makes it difficult for us to believe claims of physical abuse from children in mainstream families.

Two dramatic instances of physical child abuse that came to light in the past few years graphically illustrate that physical abuse of children can occur even in middle-class, white, apparently respectable families. One case became public because a teenage boy shot his abusing father. In that situation the abuser was an Internal Revenue Service agent.

Another egregious instance of physical child abuse was especially shocking because it was committed by a man who most people would not have suspected of being an abuser. It was the case of six-year-old Lisa Steinberg, who was subjected to several weeks of physical abuse before the battering that finally killed her in October 1987. She was abused by her adoptive father, Joel B. Steinberg, a most unlikely figure for fatal child abuse according to societal stereotypes.

The family was not poor. In fact, they lived in "a Greenwich Village neighborhood of brownstones and trendy shops" on "fashionable West 10th Street," according to an article in the *New York Times* of November 7, 1987. Joel Steinberg was an attorney—neither unemployed nor of the lower class.

## SOCIETAL FACTORS

In addition to characteristics of the parent, the child, and the family, it is necessary to consider the societal context when attempting to understand why people abuse their children. One important social attitude is the use of corporal punishment as an approved way of disciplining a child.

In Chapter 1 we described an analysis done by Dr. Katherine Christoffel of Children's Hospital in Chicago in which she found that several European countries—notably Sweden, Norway, Italy, and the Netherlands—reported little or no fatal abuse of children under four years of age. This is not due to the absence of reporting laws. But it may be because spanking and other forms of physical punishment are frowned on in those countries.

According to Dr. Christoffel, "Sweden even has a law against corporal punishment—it's illegal to hit your own child." Norway has also passed such a law.

Dr. Heins also noted the connection between a society's acceptance of corporal punishment and the occurrence of child abuse. In her 1984 article in the *Journal of the American Medical Association,* she wrote:

> Physical punishment of children is used by between 84 percent and 97 percent of all families. A recent survey of violence in American families revealed that 4 percent of children, aged 3 to 17 years, had been subjected to severe violence in the survey years, a figure that projects to between 1.2 and 2 million children per year. It is likely that even more children [than this] are subjected to violence.

Dr. Newberger supports this view. Writing in the *New England Journal of Medicine,* he said:

> Values of a society may influence methods of child rearing at home. The acceptance of corporal punishment in schools may encourage parents to use harsh discipline. In his article (published in *Critical Perspectives on Child Abuse*) 'Controlling Child Abuse in America: An Effort Doomed to Failure,' the distinguished American psychologist Edward Zigler contends that so long as corporal punishment is sanctioned, child abuse will be inevitable."

•    •    •    •

# CHAPTER 5

· · · · · · · · · · · · · · · ·

# THE DETECTION
# OF CHILD
# ABUSE

There are many ways that child abuse, both physical and sexual, comes to the attention of people who are in a position to do something about it. Besides parents, such professionals as teachers, day-care workers, high-school counselors, physicians, social workers, and others may come into contact with an abused child. These professionals are part of the "social monitoring system" for child abuse. Neighbors and family friends are other people who may see signs of abuse in children.

In addition, several American corporations have undertaken a very different approach to uncovering child abuse. Rather than depending on reports of suspected abuse by professionals, companies such as DuPont, Honeywell, and 3M are offering abusing

*A poster sponsored by the 3M Foundation, one of several large corporations that fund programs that offer counseling services to individuals who are abusing their children.*

parents an opportunity to consult confidentially with a psychologist at the workplace. These companies, which have formed a coalition called Responses to End Abuse of Children, Inc., are giving the parents a chance to seek help themselves. Because most experts in child abuse believe that many abusing parents love their children and want to stop hurting them but do not know where to get help, such programs may have a beneficial effect. For the time being, however, most abuse is detected by persons outside the family.

Organized monitoring and reporting systems for child abuse could not be established until society acknowledged the problem. In Chapter 2 we saw how, in the 1960s, Dr. C. Henry Kempe initiated a process that led to a new awareness of child abuse in America and to the establishment of many private and federal agencies to study and combat this problem.

One of the most important consequences of this new public awareness of child abuse was legislation. By 1967 all of the 50 states had passed laws making it compulsory for certain professionals to report suspected child abuse. All of these state laws obligated physicians to report under penalty. In some states teachers, clergy, attorneys, day-care workers, high school counselors, police officers, social workers, and psychologists are also obligated to report suspected child abuse. In 19 jurisdictions "any person" who suspects abuse must report it. It is important to recognize that the informant is not required to assess the probability of abuse. If a person in a profession named by law even suspects the possibility that abuse is occurring, he or she is legally obligated to report it.

To encourage reporting, these laws grant immunity from civil or criminal liability for people reporting suspected child abuse when the report is made in good faith, even if the alleged abuse is not later confirmed. Such immunity provisions have been tested in the courts and judged to be valid.

Conversely, professionals mandated to report suspected child abuse have been sued for damages in civil court for not reporting. A Maine orthopedic surgeon was brought to court in 1982 because he had not reported that he set the broken wrist of a child whose mother had hit him with a broom. In 1976 the California Supreme Court held that both failure to diagnose child abuse and failure to report it to the proper authorities constitute medical malpractice. In that case the court awarded $400,000 to a child who was permanently brain damaged by an episode of abuse subsequent to the one that the physician treated and did not report.

In 1988 a court case in Georgia suggested that public officials may be starting to take seriously reporting provisions applying to professionals other than physicians. In that case a counselor was indicted for not reporting a case of alleged abuse. This was the first indictment brought under a 1965 state law requiring psychologists, counselors, school employees, and day-care workers to report suspected child abuse. The arrest had the desired impact: In the next two days reports of suspected child abuse from professionals tripled in the county where the counselor was indicted. Reports also increased in surrounding counties. This showed that professionals knew of suspected cases but had been reluctant to report them.

Physicians and teachers are two of the most frequent and reliable sources of reports of suspected abuse. It is worth detailing some of the ways that doctors and teachers come to suspect that a child is being abused. In general, a physician would more likely come to suspect abuse while treating a child's physical injuries, while teachers would observe behavioral changes, including poor school performance and truancy.

Physicians' reports are crucial to the process of discovering and prosecuting child abusers. One reason for this is that physicians have the techniques and knowledge necessary to assess the extent of physical abuse. In addition, doctors are highly respected in American society, so a physician's report is given great credence. Sociologist Richard J. Gelles, Ph.D., of the University of Rhode Island, found in a 1978 study done for the National Center on Child Abuse and Neglect that physicians' reports are highly likely to be believed, even when a child's injuries are not severe.

Another reason reporting by physicians is so important is that they are often the only ones who can detect some forms of abuse or potential for abuse. Dr. Kempe identified two situations that he called "self-referral," in which there is a potential for abuse. Some parents repeatedly bring a healthy child to a physician, insisting the child is sick. Dr. Kempe suggested that if a parent brings a healthy child to the doctor or the emergency room twice in one day, the potential for abuse is high. The parents are using contact with the doctor as a means of asking for help. The second type of self-referral that Dr. Kempe identified is the situation in which parents consult a doctor for their own anxiety attacks or other acute psychiatric symptoms, but their real problem is fear that they will harm their child.

But more often than seeing parents who are trying to warn someone that they are about to abuse their children, doctors see injured children. When this happens, the physician will look for two factors that may be indicative of abuse: undue delay by the parent in seeking treatment for the child's injury and a discrepancy between the injury and the parent's explanation. Doctors will also take note of what type of injury the child is suffering; many types of childhood injuries have been found to be highly suggestive of abuse.

Norman Ellerstein, M.D., who works at Children's Hospital in Buffalo, New York, noted the types of skin damage that occur with abuse. He remarked that the shape of bruises can reveal

*Doctors often have excellent opportunities to detect signs of child abuse. Injuries such as fractures sustained by infants or small children are often the result of physical abuse.*

striking with a belt or cord. Also easily identified by an experienced doctor are deliberate adult human bite marks.

Broken bones can also reveal abuse. For example, some abused children have several fractures that are healing but that occurred at different times. This suggests deliberate abuse over a prolonged period of time rather than multiple, separate accidental injuries.

In young babies some types of bone injuries are almost certain signs of abuse, because an infant cannot generate enough force to cause those injuries. As Dr. James Kent, the Los Angeles psychologist who works with abused children, says, "You don't get a spiral fracture in a six-month-old baby's leg by getting his leg caught in the bars of a crib and twisting it while trying to get loose. It takes an adult to exert that much force."

In 1974 Dr. John Caffey, a radiologist, was one of the earliest physicians to speak about the physical abuse of children. Dr.

Caffey reported on a particular type of injury called whiplash shaking syndrome (WLS). This occurs when an infant is seized by the arms and rapidly and repeatedly shaken back and forth. WLS causes bleeding in the brain, which can lead to permanent brain damage and mental retardation. Another sign of WLS is bleeding from the vessels in the eyes, so-called retinal hemorrhage, which can cause blindness.

Shaking is particularly dangerous to the infant, Dr. Caffey wrote, because "the infantile head is relatively heavier and the neck muscles of infancy are weaker than at any other age level." In 1984 physicians at Children's Hospital in Philadelphia reported that "shaken baby syndrome," as they called it, is more common than popularly believed. It is important for doctors to be aware of the signs of shaking in an infant, since this form of abuse can cause severe damage without leaving any external evidence of the abuse.

Sexual abuse may be harder to recognize. Often sexual abuse leaves no apparent injury or infection; doctors are not able to detect traces of sperm unless the abuse happened recently. So it is crucial for the physician to get the maximum information from the interview with the child. The doctor should interview the child separately from the parent(s) and tape the interview so the child will not have to repeat his or her story. In a 1976 article, David L. Chadwick, M.D., of San Diego Children's Hospital emphasized that detection of child abuse requires that the doctor be alert to this possibility:

> Child abuse, as a disease, is in the same stage that venereal disease was a generation ago. The person who thinks he may have it is not eager to discuss it with anyone and is likely to approach the problem obliquely. Abused infants and children are often brought to the physician for care, but the person who brings them often comes with a complaint that has nothing to do with the obvious injury.

In 1979 surgeon Donald W. Hight, M.D., and his colleagues at the University of Michigan Medical Center reported their experience with abused children treated for burns. Of 872 youngsters admitted to the burn unit, 142, or 16%, had inflicted burns. These deliberately burned children made up almost 10% of all child abuse cases treated at the center during that time. Almost half of these children had previously been seen at the hospital for other types of deliberate injuries.

Most doctors will recognize cigarette or hot-iron burns. But diffuse scalding burns, which made up the large majority of those seen on abused children in the burn unit, can look like accidental burns. So Dr. Hight and the other doctors identified several characteristics that suggest deliberate injury.

Certain types of symmetrical, or "mirror image," burn marks seen on babies could only be made by dipping the infant's buttocks into very hot water, usually because of soiling. Inflicted burns may be more severe than accidental burns, as the abuser holds the baby's body parts in the hot water. And when the burn is inflicted by an adult, skin folds are not burned, as they would be if the child were stretched out when he or she spilled hot water. Unaffected skin folds are a sign that the baby was held while in the scalding water.

John M. Pascoe, M.D., and his colleagues, who are also from the University of Michigan, described soft-tissue injuries in abused children. Of course, muscles and other soft tissues on the body are frequently injured in accidental falls or bumps. But in abused children bruises were much more often found over the cheeks, the trunk (especially over the upper and the lower back), the genitals, the buttocks, and on the back of the upper legs. Most soft-tissue injuries due to accidents occur where a bone lies close to the skin, for instance, the knees or the shins.

What can a doctor do if he or she suspects abuse? Here are a few simple steps suggested in a 1984 report on child abuse by the American Medical Association:

- The physician should consider discussing with the parents the fact that child maltreatment is in the differential diagnosis of the problem. During such a discussion, the physician should remain objective and avoid accusatory or judgmental statements to the parents.

- The doctor must keep a record of all pertinent data in the medical chart, which may be an essential part of court proceedings. Recording exact details is very important. Because it can take a long time for abuse cases to get to court, physicians and nurses should not rely on memory but should chart the signs of physical abuse on an outline of the body.

57

> • It is the physician's responsibility to protect the child from further harm, either by referring the case to an agency or by putting the child into the hospital.

Unfortunately, the great potential to pick up possible child abuse cases in the doctor's office often is lost, because doctors either do not recognize the signs of abuse or they do not report suspected abuse. One study, reported in the medical newspaper *Medical Post* in 1985, found that physicians often do not report abuse cases because they think that abused children are not seen in private physicians' offices. Fear of losing patients was another reason given by some doctors.

David Fisher, J.D., a Pittsburgh attorney who works to protect the rights of abused children, agrees that physicians need to be more diligent in detecting and reporting child abuse. In the March 1976 issue of the journal *Pediatric Annals* he wrote, "Physicians, particularly physicians in private practice, are the chief obstacle to the effective reporting of child abuse and neglect under the reporting laws." He cited several reasons why this is so. In addition to those we have already mentioned, he listed doctors' feelings that "reporting to public child welfare agencies [is] futile because the agencies are overloaded with work, understaffed, and generally ineffective in treating and managing abuse and neglect cases."

*In some states, police are obligated to report any case of suspected child abuse.*

Dr. Fisher suggested this solution:

> Perhaps the most effective method of encouraging reporting by professionals is the development of the interdisciplinary team approach as it has now evolved in many children's hospitals and child protection agencies. On presentation of certain injuries, histories, or inconsistencies, a meeting of the interdisciplinary team is convened to review the case. Physicians, psychologists, psychiatrists, nurses, social workers, lawyers, police, clergy, and teachers may constitute the team. Together they can explore the situation comprehensively to determine the possibility of abuse and plan for management of the case.

One such multidisciplinary unit is the Child Protection Team (CPT) at New York Hospital. Organized by the pediatrician Daniel B. Kessler, M.D., in 1983, the team consists of a pediatrician, a social worker, and a resident doctor who completes a fellowship in child protection. A psychologist, a psychiatrist, and pediatric nurses are also available for consultations. Dr. Kessler estimates that there are now "several hundred" such teams at hospitals in the United States, a development that he terms "relatively recent."

Members of the team function at several levels. Primary responsibility resides with the resident doctor or fellow, who provides consultation to other doctors in the hospital on an emergency basis. In Dr. Kessler's experience, calls to the CPT come from three main sources: the emergency room, the burn center, and children admitted for another problem from whom a doctor, nurse, or social worker elicits a history that suggests abuse.

The fellow may advise a doctor by phone how to do a thorough examination for abuse or which records or reports need to be filed, and whether a child should be admitted to the hospital. Sometimes the fellow may see the child personally. Dr. Kessler is on hand for backup and to help with complicated evaluations. Some of the most difficult cases involve failure to thrive, which can require considerable medical expertise and consultation with doctors in several specialties.

Equally important, the fellow and other members of the CPT have legal knowledge as well as medical knowledge. They know what physicians can and must do in cases of suspected child abuse, and they know that a child must be hospitalized if anyone suspects that the child would be in "imminent danger" if returned to the home setting.

A member of the team can inform a doctor in the emergency room, for example, that the hospital has a legal right to hold the child in protective custody, but a hospital representative must notify the appropriate child protection agency that they have done so, and it may be advisable to notify the police. CPT members also know that parents can challenge protective custody in court, and that a doctor must respond at the hearing with the reasons why abuse was suspected and why the child was admitted.

The court may uphold the hospital's judgment or order the child released in the custody of the parents. But even if the child goes back to the parents the hospital will not be penalized if there were valid reasons for suspecting danger. It is the job of CPT members to know what those grounds are. Another reason to be prudent about taking children into the hospital for protective custody is that, if the court upholds custody, the law requires that the child be detained until appropriate placement can be arranged. That may necessitate a costly hospitalization.

CPT members also undertake outreach work with private physicians in the community, alerting them to the existence of the CPT and to the signs of child abuse. "Doctors in private practice are less likely to call in suspected child abuse to the central registry because of social and economic reasons," Dr. Kessler says. For instance, the reporting doctor may end up spending many hours in court, which is time lost from his or her practice. But if community doctors know about the CPT at the hospital and have actually met the CPT fellow or social worker or Dr. Kessler, they are more likely to call the team directly or send a child to the emergency room when they suspect abuse. As a result of this liaison work, says Dr. Kessler, "calls from outside the hospital have been happening more frequently."

One unfortunate aspect of this work, Dr. Kessler says, is that members of the CPT "drop out much too early in the process." Once a case is taken over by the city, state, or county child protection services agency, further findings become confidential, and even Dr. Kessler and the other members of his team cannot find out the outcome of the evaluation. At one time the social worker on the New York Hospital Child Protection Team set out to do follow-up of cases that the team reported, but it turned out to be a nearly impossible task to track the disposition of reports or to know if an adequate evaluation had been done. While acknowledging the value of confidentiality, Dr. Kessler feels that child protection agency social workers "sometimes hide behind issues of confidentiality."

Dr. Kessler acknowledges that lack of feedback from the system can turn doctors off from reporting. "It's discouraging for professionals who make reports to the state," he says. "They often say, 'Why did I do that?' They end up seeing the system as unresponsive."

## Other Detection Sources

Of the other professionals obligated to report suspected child abuse, teachers are a particularly valuable source of reports. This is because a teacher sees a child almost every day for a long period of time. If there are changes in the child's behavior—and behavioral changes usually do accompany physical or sexual abuse—teachers will often perceive them. The next step would then involve calling in a county child protective services worker

*Any adult who suspects a case of child abuse should not only contact the proper authorities but also offer support and understanding to the child.*

to carry out an evaluation. Overall, school personnel have an outstanding reporting record.

If young persons cannot get an adult whom they know to listen to their story and believe it, they do have another option. A child or adolescent can call the National Child Abuse Hotline: 1–800–422–4453. Staffed by trained clinical psychologists, the hot line takes calls from abused children looking for help, as well as from people who want to report suspected abuse and parents who are afraid they might abuse their child and want help. About one in four callers is a child.

After the hot-line counselor talks at length with the child, explaining what child protection services are, the counselor calls a local social worker, who will join the counselor and the child in a conference call. The social worker will then go to the school or the home to meet the child apart from the parents. Together, the social worker and the child may figure out the next step.

Unfortunately, even otherwise responsible adults do not always fulfill their responsibility to report incidents of child abuse. Dr. Gloria Bachmann found that even when a child makes an abusive incident known, at least 10% of adults fail to respond. After the 1987 beating death of six-year-old Lisa Steinberg in New York, neighbors admitted they had suspected something. A downstairs neighbor says she was worried by the girl's appearance but failed to do anything. "I hadn't any evidence at all," she told a *New York Times* reporter. "What could I do?"

According to the reporter, "A new round of interviews with neighbors of the family revealed that many, though concerned, did nothing. A combination of fear, apathy and a big-city reluctance to breach another family's privacy apparently prevented them from alerting the authorities."

•    •    •    •    •

# CHAPTER 6

· · · · · · · · · · · · · · · ·

# WHO WILL PROTECT THE CHILDREN?

Once a child protection agency gets a report of a case of suspected child abuse, the staff initiates a series of steps to evaluate the charge, protect the child during the evaluation, and, if the allegation is true, to treat both the child and the abuser.

Courts may become involved in this series of steps in two ways. First, a judge may be asked to curtail parental rights—that is, restrict the abusive parent or parents from seeing the child—temporarily or permanently to allow protective custody of the child or placement in a foster home during the initial evaluation

*Dr. Anne Harris Cohen is the Director of the National Committee for the Prevention of Child Abuse, one of several organizations involved in the fight against child abuse.*

or treatment. Second, criminal charges may be brought against the abuser.

As we saw in the last chapter, there are a number of people—professional and otherwise—who are responsible for reporting suspected cases of child abuse. After bringing the case to someone's attention, these people are then required to fill out a written report on the suspected abuse. Upon receipt of a report, the county social service agency has a legal mandate to investigate promptly (usually within 24 to 48 hours), to supply immediate protection for the child from further harm, to furnish treatment for existing injuries, to provide services to the child and family when the investigation reveals abusive treatment, and to seek court intervention for authority to act or to determine what action is appropriate.

To carry out these mandates, a social service worker is assigned to investigate the charge as soon as the child welfare agency receives it. If the social worker decides that the child is in danger in the home, he or she initiates a preventive custody motion. At the custody hearing, a judge decides whether the child is indeed in danger. The judge can then order a parental evaluation or immediate treatment for both the parents and the child.

In many states, the court allows the child to be removed from the home until a custody hearing can take place. Whether or not a state allows summary removal without court judgment, when the custody hearing occurs rules of evidence are similar in most states. The state does not have to prove that anyone specific is an offender. Representatives of the children only need to show two things: (1) that the child was injured or molested; and (2) that the parents cannot offer a reasonable and satisfactory explanation for the injury or molestation. This establishes a case of neglect on the parents' part, which is adequate for removing the child from the home, at least temporarily.

There are several possible courses of action if a judge determines that a child is in danger in the home. The judge may allow the child to remain with his or her parents, but under the supervision of a social worker who makes periodic visits to the home to ensure the child's safety. If the abuser is an after-school caretaker, such as a working mother's boyfriend, the department of family services may pay for after-school care, as well as a child psychologist or psychiatrist. If the home environment is threatening, the child may be placed temporarily in a foster home or sent to live for a time with a relative.

When the social service agency's evaluation substantiates the charge of child abuse, the agency acquires additional obligations. It must develop a treatment program for the family, which will consist of some combination of financial aid, homemaker services, social worker home visits, and family therapy. The purpose of this treatment program is to alleviate the family and home stress that led to child abuse.

For the long term, the child protection agency is charged with what is called "permanency planning," which refers to the final settlement of the case in a way that best serves the abused child's interests. Depending on the results of family therapy and treatment for the abused child, options for long-term care include leaving the child in the home, reuniting him with his parents (if he has been taken out of the home), removing him from the home (if he has been left in the home), referral to the state adoption agency, appointment of a legal guardian, long-term foster care, or, in the case of some teenagers, emancipation (declaring the teenager a legal adult, although he or she may be 1 or 2 years under 18).

Removing the child from the home is a drastic step and is usually taken only when it is suspected that the parent or parents will not change their abusive behavior. In these cases the state must prove that the child was abused and that the danger of continued abuse persists.

Many people argue, however, that reporting cases of child abuse interferes with the parents' right to privacy. As for the seeming conflict between the right of the child to a safe and healthy life and the right of the parents to privacy, Dr. Kempe had this to say:

> Where the state is supreme, this particular problem is easily managed: in a dictatorship each child belongs to the state and you may not damage state property. The really first-rate attention paid to the health of all children in less free societies makes you wonder whether one of our cherished democratic freedoms is the right to maim our own children. When I brought this question to the attention of one of our judges, he said, "That may be the price we have to pay." Who pays the price? Nobody has asked the child.

## Therapy for Abused Children

Once a social work evaluation is done and abuse is verified, one of the most important responses is psychological therapy for the child. One form of treatment is "talk therapy," sessions in which the abused child and a therapist meet one-on-one to help the child make sense of what happened and to help the child understand that he or she is not at fault.

Dr. Kent points out that one particularly difficult aspect of therapy for sexually abused children is that they have learned prematurely how pleasurable sex is. The therapist needs to acknowledge that it was all right for the youngster to feel pleasure: "You're not bad for feeling that" should be the message, "but the person who made you engage in sexual acts did a bad thing."

There are currently some innovative options to psychotherapy for children who have been physically abused. One of these options is therapeutic day care. In therapeutic day care an abused child who is living in foster care spends the day in a supervised situation much like commercial day care with one major difference—the abusive parent is present as well. Therapists observe interactions between parent and child in a situation that is more like day-to-day life than a therapist's office. "Therapeutic daycare provides lots of child-parent contact in a case where you may be nervous about leaving the child in the home," Dr. Kent explains. Therefore, it creates a situation somewhere between complete foster care and leaving the child at home.

Dr. Kent notes that although there were once 14 or 15 programs like this around the country, most have closed down for want of money. This is clearly because these programs are both labor- and money-intensive. Nonetheless, professionals in the field regard this mode of treatment very highly and are trying to

*Perhaps the most crucial response to child abuse is providing emotional therapy for the victim.*

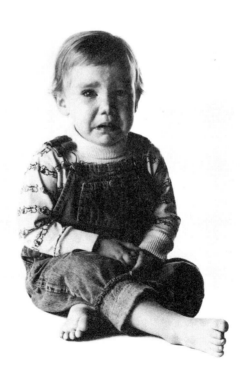

keep it going. In fact, Dr. Kent and his colleagues at the Children's Evaluation Center are currently in the process of setting up such a program.

Dr. Kent also described an even more ambitious and innovative program for physically abused children in the Netherlands. This program, a residential treatment program, puts both abused children and their parents together as a family unit in a residence, where they live together and are treated together. Such a situation can offer very intensive observation and treatment. Residential treatment is based on the assumption that there are triggers in family interactions that set off abusive behavior. Counselors can observe and identify these triggering elements and try to alter such behavior.

## Therapy for Abusers

Group therapy is sometimes used for treatment of sexual offenders. Several years ago counselor Hank Giarretto, of San Jose, California, set up therapy workshops for couples. Men who had sexually molested their daughters attended, along with their wives. This form of therapy has grown into a nationwide organization called Parents United. "It helps adults, victims and offenders alike, to cope with the consequences of child molestation," Giarretto says.

The prevailing attitude toward rehabilitation of sexual offenders was expressed in a 1984 article in *Newsweek* by Dr. A. Nicholas Groth, former director of the program for child molesters at the state prison in Somers, Connecticut: "We look at it like an alcohol-abuse problem. We don't think there's a cure for it, but you can learn to control it." Psychiatrist Gene Abel, M.D., of the Behavioral Medicine Institute in Atlanta, is one therapist who believes that sex offenders can be taught to control their impulses. In a program that Dr. Abel devised and ran, 82% of sexual offenders stopped their child molestation. Among all types of sexual offenders, Dr. Abel says, incest is "the easiest to treat."

In Dr. Abel's treatment program, the most time is spent focusing on decreasing the adult's sexual interest in children. The adult is taught to use aversive images when he is in a tempting situation. These adverse images can be mind pictures in which the molestation of children is coupled with unpleasant associa-

*Dr. Bill Hobson, director of the program for child molesters at the state prison in Somers, Connecticut. The main goal of such programs is not to "cure" molesters but to help them control their impulses.*

tions. Other steps in the treatment are to help the adult molester to deal with adults socially and sexually (many sexually offending men are married) and to change the false beliefs with which they justify their sexual interest in children.

Dr. Abel is now turning his attention to treatment of adolescent sexual molesters. During therapy sessions Dr. Abel found that most adult offenders started molesting younger children before the age of 18. Consequently, this has given therapists a new opportunity to prevent many future cases of child abuse if an adolescent molester can be successfully treated.

A more controversial approach to treating repeat sexual offenders is drug therapy. Doctors at Johns Hopkins University in Baltimore have been giving Depo-Provera, a drug containing a female hormone that reduces male sexual desire, to male sex offenders. In 1984 a judge in Kalamazoo, Michigan, ordered that the drug be administered to Robert Gauntlett, 42, the great-grandson of the founder of the Upjohn Co., a large pharmaceutical firm, because he molested his stepdaughter.

Other useful treatment programs available to parents who abuse their children are parent education classes and skill development classes in such areas as household management, health care, and vocational skills development.

One intervention that has proved to be a particularly effective form of therapy for abusive parents is Parents Anonymous. This program is designed to provide help and support to parents who fear they may become abusive.

## The Outcome

But what becomes of the children who have been abused? Although studies show that some, in turn, will abuse their children, others have risen above their history of abuse and gone on to become successful, giving adults.

Dr. Richard Krugman of the Kempe Center in Denver is particularly interested in the question of the future of abused children. "About two-thirds of abused children become adult survivors," Dr. Krugman says. "Many of them have children and are doing very well with them. I think that's very optimistic. That tells me that those people had a therapeutic intervention of some kind." Dr. Krugman's conclusion is that "there is a great deal we can do to prevent that cycle [of recurrent child abuse] from continuing."

What is the difference between abused children who grow up to become abusers and those who do not? Dr. Krugman says that two important elements contribute to a positive outcome:

1. The child learns that the abuse was not his or her fault.

2. The child finds other important adult role models.

Therefore, it is possible that intensive therapy is not always needed for a child to survive and flourish. In fact, all that may be needed is support and care, and a great deal of understanding.

•        •        •        •

# CHAPTER 7

. . . . . . . . . . . . . .

# THE ABUSED CHILD AND THE COURTS

**R**eporting a suspected case of child abuse sets into motion two quite distinct reactions. The first is the protection of the child followed by therapy for both the abused child and the abusive parent or parents. The other common result is criminal prosecution of the abuser. Some children's rights advocates believe that court proceedings are actually detrimental to the child's rehabilitation and that treatment of the child cannot begin until a trial is over. Consequently, the question of whether to prosecute has become a major conflict in the field.

Dr. David Chadwick of San Diego argues that criminal prosecution is a waste of effort that would best be applied to other areas. "Few communities can afford to waste resources on ineffective 'therapeutic' measures such as criminal prosecution," he points out. "Still, many communities do waste their efforts in this way, while failing to provide adequate child protective services, hot-lines for stressed parents, intensive support of possible abusers, and other preventive measures."

On the other side of the argument are people like Jim Peters, a former prosecutor and a senior attorney with the National Center for the Prosecution of Child Abuse. "There is a whole school of social work that says that physical abuse within the family should not be criminal," Peters notes. But, he argues, "there is no moral or legal justification for doing something to your own child that you would be prosecuted for if you did to someone else's kid."

For the present, prosecutors like Jim Peters make the decisions, and many child abuse cases go to court. An appearance in court, however, often raises additional problems for the abused child. Child abuse is a great enough tragedy in itself. But, as often happens with rape, when the victim enters the judicial system there may well be a further battering. Unfortunately, the U.S. court system does not always seem to treat children kindly. It operates under an adversary system, in which attorneys are allowed to cross-examine witnesses brutally, without regard to their feelings. Such a system may work with adults, although even sensitive adults can break down under the onslaught of a badgering defense attorney.

When the person being put through the third-degree examination is 5 or even 14 years old, the callous nature of the adversary judicial system becomes acutely obvious. Even when one parent is accusing the other of abusing a child, the defending parent may instruct his or her attorney to use all permissible intimidation to shake his or her own child's testimony.

Emotional traumatization of children in the courtroom has become a greater problem recently because an increasing number of cases are being brought to trial. Unfortunately, cases of child abuse may be dismissed because a child witness becomes confused and upset under this cross-examination, or parents will decline to bring a case to trial to spare their child the stress of courtroom trauma.

There are many current attempts to solve this problem. One approach is to rely on other witnesses in addition to the abused child. Testimony can come from the professional who first interviewed the child, or from the adult to whom the child first confided the alleged abuse. This would allow the jury to have the benefit of the child's freshest recollection.

One obstacle to this approach is that such secondhand testimony obtained at pretrial hearings is considered hearsay and is not admissible as evidence. However, such evidence may be crucial or may indeed be the only testimony in a particular case. Recent judicial reforms have allowed judges in child abuse trials to admit hearsay evidence if they feel that the child's presence in court would result in psychological damage. Judges are also now more liberal in allowing as evidence statements made at the initial interview.

Another popular option consists of legislation that makes it unnecessary for a child to actually testify in court or to be cross-examined by a defense attorney. Shielding a child abuse victim from the trauma of litigation while protecting the defendant's right to confront his accuser is a tricky business. Seventeen states have tried to safeguard the rights of both the child and the accused with so-called shield laws, which allow children to testify via closed-circuit television or videotape.

Ideally, with this method the child would never have to give testimony while directly facing or being in the presence of the abuser, a person who is linked with traumatic experiences in the child's mind. Children may be frightened to report the abuse and terrified at the thought of facing this person in court despite the assurance of police and child protection services workers.

But on June 29, 1988, the U.S. Supreme Court struck down one type of shield law in the case of *Coy v. Iowa*. In the process they reversed an Iowa man's conviction for molesting two 13-year-old girls, ruling that the use of a one-way screen to shield the victims from having to look at the defendant when they testified violated his constitutional right to confront his accusers face-to-face.

How extensively will this ruling affect prosecution of alleged child abusers? Attorney Peters notes that "Iowa was the only state that had a law calling for a translucent barrier" in court during testimony. So the immediate impact of the court's ruling will be very limited. But, he says, in the 17 states that have one-way closed-circuit statutes (allowing testimony to be viewed on closed-circuit TV) that also allow a judge to call for taping, "those statutes are probably in serious danger."

Whatever the constitutional outcome, the National Center for the Prosecution of Child Abuse continues to advocate children testifying in their own cases. "With sensitive preparation and experienced prosecutors, most kids can testify," says Peters.

When a child does testify, testimony must be handled in such a way that the child is not further traumatized. This is best done by briefing the child on what to expect in the courtroom so he or she is not shocked into silence. Says Dr. Krugman, "We need attorneys in this country to think about how to help children when they interact with the courts."

Since court appearances will continue to be necessary, someone is needed to help children during trials. Although the states' child protective services workers are supposed to represent a child's best interests in court, most are swamped. Caseworkers can average caseloads as high as 60 children at one time.

A program called Court-Appointed Special Advocates (C-ASA) has been formed to solve this problem. Before court, C-ASA volunteers provide background information that can aid attorneys in presenting their cases. During court proceedings, the volunteer acts as hand-holder, explaining to an often confused and frightened child what is happening while encouraging the child to express him- or herself. The volunteer also helps shape the recommendations for whether the child should remain at home, be placed in foster care, or be freed for adoption by severing parental ties.

As difficult as court appearances may be for victims of physical abuse, it is of an entirely different magnitude with victims of sexual abuse. In cases of child sexual abuse there is often no physical evidence of sexual molestation. The child's testimony can be virtually the only evidence. Consequently, the defense tries especially hard to discredit the child's assertions. Often, it may appear to be a classic case of adding insult to injury: A girl may have been molested by her father or stepfather for years, and she is then accused of inventing the whole story.

In addition to being branded a liar by the defense attorney, who at least has a clear motive, the sexually abused child is often doubted even by those who have no stake in the trial. Some people

*CASA (Court Appointed Special Advocates): Volunteers offer support to abused and neglected children throughout the entire trial period.*

simply do not give credence to a child's allegations of sexual abuse. And when a girl says that her respectable middle-class father did the molesting, her problem is compounded by our society's myth that nice men simply do not do such things.

Even when children do not invent such charges themselves, some people say, they can be coached to make the charges. One situation in which this might happen is a divorce and custody hearing. Some lawyers believe that this is a potentially common problem. Defense attorney Ed Tolley, of Athens, Georgia, says, "In every divorce case there is now a potential child abuse case, with a discontented spouse alleging child abuse for the purpose of gaining a leg up in the domestic litigation."

The facts, however, do not support this view. A joint study by the American Bar Association's Child Advocacy Center and the Association of Family and Conciliation Courts, published in 1988, concluded that "there is no reason to believe that allegations [of sexual abuse] are false simply because they arise after a custody hearing has begun." The survey also found that the percentage

*Anatomically correct dolls are often used to help victims of sexual abuse make themselves understood.*

of sexual abuse charges that arise during divorce or custody disputes is extremely small.

Several tools are available to help investigate alleged sexual abuse. One aid is anatomically correct dolls, which help children show in detail what happened to them when they are too young to have the necessary vocabulary or when they are reluctant to talk about it.

Dr. Abigail Sivan, a member of the Section of Child Psychiatry at the Rush Presbyterian-St. Luke's Medical Center in Chicago, points out that nonabused children act differently with these dolls. "The [nonabused] children showed little aggression and displayed no explicit sexual activity in their play with these dolls," she reported. "This is in direct contrast with observed behavior of sexually abused children in which both aggressive activity and sexual precocity are seen.

"The study indicates that investigators should take seriously any unusual behaviors a child shows in his or her play with the dolls as an indication that the child has some sort of problem that should be explored."

Another way to find out whether a child has been abused is to have him or her draw a human body. Abused children frequently produce drawings with grossly exaggerated genitals, omitted appendages, and other distortions.

Psychological tests, too, are helpful. According to Dr. Kempe, "projective psychological tests reveal that incest victims see themselves as defenseless, worthless, guilty, at risk and threatened from all sides, particularly from their father and mother who would be expected to be their protectors. . . . Projective tests clearly differentiate the angry, wrongful accuser from the rather depressed incestuous victim."

The child's story, play with dolls, drawings, and psychological tests can be supplemented by signs of emotional disturbance in the child. These usually take the form of secrecy, a decline in school performance, precocious knowledge of sexual acts, seductive behavior, bed-wetting and nightmares, and role reversal (playing parent instead of child).

## Alternatives

There are ways to avoid going to court when dealing with charges of sexual abuse. An alternative approach was used recently in England when widespread allegations of child sexual abuse were made in a midsize northern town. In England, children can be summarily removed from the home for 28 days if a physician believes abuse has taken place. This is done under a "Place of Safety" order, a procedure created by the 1969 Children's Act.

In 1986, in the town of Cleveland, England, 76 children were removed from their homes under Place of Safety proceedings.

*Kee McFarlane of the Children's Institute International uses puppets to help an abused child open up and tell his story.*

During the first half of 1987, however, 202 children were removed. The difference: A new physician had come to the town who was specially trained in recognizing child sexual abuse. Eventually half of the children were released, but doctors maintained that 95 children had actually been abused.

Questions arose, however, over whether these charges were all true. Upset parents formed an organization called Parents Against Injustice and received a sympathetic hearing in the press, which portrayed them not as villains but as the helpless victims of overzealous doctors.

Amid all this controversy, the British system responded quite differently from the American system. The issue was not settled by lawsuits or criminal prosecutions in court. Rather, the health minister set up a judicial inquiry to investigate the affair. Early in the inquiry it was decided that the children would not testify during the proceedings. Instead, details of what the children suffered were passed on by lawyers.

In July 1988, the board issued its findings, called the Butler-Sloss Report. They found that a large number of the allegations had been accurate. Ironically, some of the cases had occurred in families in which the father, the alleged molester, had most loudly protested his innocence.

Rather than ending with uncertainty, frustration, doubts, prison terms, and lawsuits, as often happens in the United States, the British situation led to suggestions for reforms in child abuse reporting laws. Two notable examples:

- The interests of the child in suspected abuse cases are to be considered above all else, starting from a general principle that children should be believed and their disclosures treated sensitively and confidentially.

- Staff working with suspected abuse cases are to be given full support and backing.

Certainly these two principles have been put forth by American experts. The difference is that in England they came from an official government inquiry board and so have a greater chance of being put into practice.

• • • •

# CHAPTER 8

. . . . . . . . . . . . . . . . . . . .

# PREVENTING CHILD ABUSE

These past 22 years have demonstrated that some combination of public health nurses, homemakers, parents aides, Parents Anonymous, direct counseling and good medical care can improve the outcome for parents at greatest risk and their children.

Yet every one of these services has been curtailed. . . . The military development of space currently is getting more attention than our children and their families.

—Dr. Ray E. Helfer, professor of pediatrics, Michigan State University, 1984.

Preventing child abuse is a course of action that is far preferable to treating its victims. Unfortunately, it is very difficult to secure money to design, test, and implement prevention programs. At a conference in the mid-1980s, Professor Charles Strickland of Emory University called for "fewer dollars for international violence and more for prevention of domestic violence." So far such calls have met with limited success. What needs to be done to change this situation? At its most fundamental level, preventing child abuse requires understanding the situation from both sides of the equation; that is, identifying and counseling the potential abuser and protecting the child.

Certainly one useful way to prevent abuse is to teach children to protect themselves. Many demonstration projects of this type are in progress. Two examples are

- In Georgia many public schools feature a puppet show that informs children about child abuse, how to avoid it, and what to do when it happens.
- The National Assault Prevention Center has initiated 250 Child Abuse Prevention projects around the country that use trained local volunteers to conduct hour-long workshops in schools. Using role-playing techniques, children learn how to protect themselves, how to avoid abusive situations, and how to exercise their rights.

More programs are needed, however, that focus on family situations that lead to abuse. It is neither fair nor effective to put pressure on children to prevent abuse. Sociologist Robert L. Burgess of Pennsylvania State University believes that we must implement programs to reduce the tendency of adults to abuse their children. Burgess advocates more prenatal (before birth) support for parents (especially younger parents) to prepare them for child care in advance. "This would involve changes in hospital practices to encourage bonding, educating parents as to what can be expected of a child at a certain age, and teaching ways to discipline," he says. Nutrition, financial management, job training, and social skills training could also benefit such parents.

There are already some simple programs of this type. Such programs offer services to parents who are judged most likely to abuse their children. Persons who may not be successful as par-

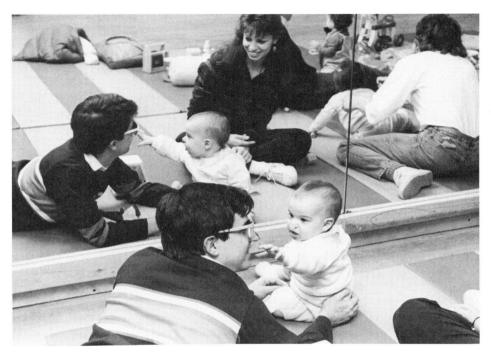

*New parents with their baby at a parent development class. Such classes guide parents through the rigors of child care so that they can cope with the frustrations as well as enjoy the pleasures of parenthood.*

ents, even though they may have a normal infant, are identified either during pregnancy or around the time of birth and given special help and support.

The ability of such an approach to make a difference in a child's life is one of the most promising developments in the field of child abuse. As early as 1978, Dr. Kempe wrote in the *American Journal of Diseases of Children*, "I am happy to say that a number of studies have now shown very clearly that child abuse is often predictable, and, in its most serious form, largely preventable."

Some of the programs providing such evidence are

- A study at Vanderbilt University, conducted during the mid-1970s, showed that increased contact between mother and infant through rooming-in service in the newborn setting can materially reduce the incidence of child abuse in the first year of life.

- At the medical center of the University of North Carolina at Chapel Hill, it was possible to identify during the mother's postbirth stay in a high-risk, intensive-care nursery those premature infants who were at highest risk of abuse by their parents.

- At the University of Rochester, David L. Olds, M.D., and his colleagues set up a program of prenatal and infancy home visits by pediatric nurse-practitioners for women who were having their first child and who were either teenagers, unmarried, or of low socioeconomic status. Among the women at highest risk for care-giving problems, those whom nurses visited had fewer instances of verified child abuse and neglect during the first two years of their children's life, punished and restricted their children less frequently, and provided more appropriate play materials.

- In a study conducted at the University of Colorado Medical Center in the mid-1970s by Dr. Kempe and his colleagues, nurses observed the behavior of parents toward newborns during labor and delivery and during the first day or two of life in the nursery. Their conclusions were highly accurate in predicting abuse in the early years of life. "Nurses' observations clearly identify those families who are in need of extra services," Dr. Kempe said.

The program at the University of Colorado is worth looking at in some detail because of the success of its intervention component. Nurses formed their impression of the parents by asking themselves some simple questions relating to mother-baby interaction directly after birth:

- How does the mother look?
- What does the mother say?
- What does the mother do?
- If the father is present, what are his reactions?

Nurses also observed the way parents touched, held, and talked to the baby. Did the parents, particularly the mother, use an affectionate tone of voice, or did they make hostile or disparaging comments about the baby's appearance? Did they make eye contact with the baby? Was there a mutually reinforcing interaction between parents or a combative or nonsupportive interaction?

Based on these observations, Dr. Kempe and his associates identified 100 families out of the first 350 observed who were in need of extra services. Half were assigned to the intervention group and half to the nonintervention group. Intervention consisted of a single pediatrician who provided personalized care with liberal access by telephone, as well as outreach services through visiting nurses and lay health visitors (often mothers eager to share their own experiences) during the two years after birth. According to Dr. Kempe, "The ideal candidate [for a lay visitor] is a successful mother who is able and interested in sharing her experience and goodwill with less experienced young families."

During the next two years the study compared the health of the children in the high-risk group—both those whose parents received intervention and those who did not—to a group of babies judged to be at low risk of abuse. This contrast showed that

*A nurse observes a new mother care for her child in her home. Home visits such as the one shown here have proven to be effective in lessening the incidence of child abuse in high-risk cases.*

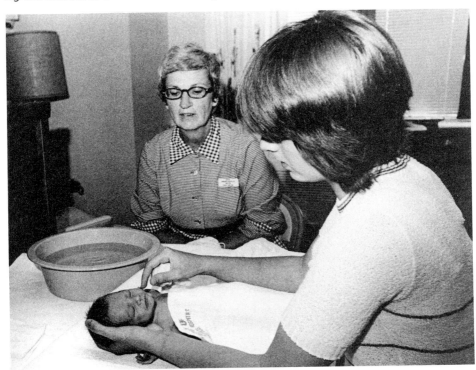

some children in the high-risk groups were abused, even with intervention. "But," said Dr. Kempe, "the most important single observation was that no child in the low-risk group and no child in the high-risk intervention group suffered an inflicted injury serious enough to require hospitalization, while five children in the high-risk non-intervention group required in-patient treatment for serious injuries."

This outcome suggests strongly that simple observations by maternity nurses coupled with benefits for parents judged to be likely to have difficulty parenting is an effective way to reduce severe child abuse. As to the price, Dr. Kempe estimates that the program cost $12,000, mostly in staff time, and saved $1 million in medical costs.

Home visitors like those in the Colorado program also exist in many European countries, but in Europe the visitors are all trained nurses. Dr. Eli Newberger, of Boston's Children's Hospital, believes that such programs are effective. In the *New England Journal of Medicine*, he wrote:

> Child abuse is not inevitable. Governments can have an important role in its perpetuation or its eradication. Countries with universal health-care systems in which the programs for maternal and infant care include regular visits by a nurse during infancy appear to prevent child abuse more effectively.

An advantage of the American approach is that lay visitors already have access and intimate knowledge of the community where they come from and in which they will serve. In addition, in Europe the emphasis is on mother-crafting skills rather than feelings and expressions of affection for the baby. Also, European visitors are not very emphatic about offering services to families who initially refuse.

Dr. Kempe believed that health visitors, as a form of effective, comprehensive health care, should be a right for all children and families, just as compulsory, universal schooling is a right. "To my mind, only a universal program will develop quality and be successful," he said.

Currently the perinatal intervention program in Denver has adopted the principle of universal home health visitation. Dr.

Krugman, the director of the Kempe Center, says that their "community caring project" has home visitors go to "as many first-time parents as we can get to." They have abandoned the concept of identifying high-risk parents because people do not usually want to know if they are considered a high risk. The Kempe Center has now convinced three hospitals in Denver to provide home health visitors as part of the hospital's child/parent education services.

In view of the success of the home health visitors, the National Committee for the Prevention of Child Abuse has set a goal to supply all new parents with support services at the time of birth or before. The committee asks its local chapters to sponsor in-hospital programs to teach first-time mothers child care skills, offer emotional support, give practical homemaking help, and help new mothers understand what they can realistically expect from their baby.

In addition to intervention at or near the time of birth, it may also be possible to reduce child abuse by intervening later, when the family is under stress but before abuse occurs. Crisis intervention services could include hot lines, respite child care, community services such as homemaking help, and parent support groups. A social component might be to raise public awareness through media messages with the theme, "Parenting is a tough job."

Unfortunately, social service agencies are swamped trying to deal with cases of abuse that already exist. Thus far, there has been a lack of staff, facilities, and, most seriously, funding—all desperately needed to put such an effort into practice. A recent proposal for such an agency was put forward in 1988 in the wake of several instances of maltreatment of children in New York City, most notably the death of 6-year-old Lisa Steinberg (see Chapter 4). New York City comptroller Harrison J. Goldin recommended the formation of a Department for Children. Writing in the *New York Times*, Mr. Goldin said: "It is time to recognize that the number and severity of [the recent disasters involving children in New York City] imply a structural failing of society and the New York City government to protect our most innocent and defenseless citizens: children. That failing can best be redressed locally through the creation of a Department for Children."

*Parents who learn to communicate with their children and to talk about problems are less likely to be abusive.*

Such an agency would be solely accountable for the administration of programs that serve and protect children. Currently that responsibility is only one task of a huge superagency, the Human Resources Administration. Mr. Goldin likened the proposed Department for Children to the city's recently created Department for the Aging. It could, he suggested, mandate a child abuse curriculum for all pediatricians in training, as well as courses for teachers in recognizing and reporting abuse.

Proposals such as this may signal a new willingness to address the problems of abused children. At this time there does appear to be an expanded awareness of this issue. For example, there has been a significant increase in press coverage of child abuse cases, the publication of books dealing with the myths surrounding child abuse, and the acceptance of sexual abuse as a topic for television and movies.

We can see the evidence of that new attitude in many cultural events. For instance, in 1984 there was a television show called "Something About Amelia," which told the story of a father's sexual molestation of his young daughter. It was a revolutionary event when it was broadcast. A 1980 song called "Hell Is For Children," by pop musician Pat Benatar, expressed the anger engendered by child abuse. And a more recent song, "Luka," by Suzanne Vega, was a vignette about a specific person, according to the singer. Particularly poignant is the song's refrain, which depicts the hopeless state that abused youngsters can get into: "You just don't argue anymore."

One of the most important recent events that has brought abuse of children more into the open in our society was the public revelation by a United States senator that she was sexually molested as a child. In 1984 Congress held hearings on child sexual abuse. At those hearings Senator Paula Hawkins of Florida stunned her colleagues and the rest of the country by openly announcing that she had to deal with the problem as a child.

Senator Hawkins related that she and many of the other young children in her neighborhood often played at the house of an elderly couple who lived there. The man was described as "a respected grandfatherly type." When the mothers had to go to the store or on other errands, they often left their young children in the care of this couple.

One day, without any preamble, the man took five-year-old Paula on his lap, gave her some candy, and immediately put his hand into her panties. Luckily the child had been warned not to let anyone touch her "in the bathing suit area." She ran home and told her mother what had happened. Her parents believed her story, and appropriate action was taken against the molester.

*A happy family gathers around the piano. Less fortunate children who have been abused can, through psychotherapy, grow up to experience the joys of close family relationships.*

It is only with such courageous, honest, and open recognition of the problem of child abuse that we can begin to understand its roots and to attempt to formulate methods of stopping it when it arises, healing the children who have been victims of it, and ultimately preventing it from occurring. As Senator Hawkins said in a newspaper interview, "I was shocked when a trained counselor seeking my help whispered to me [about the problem]. It's a subject that must be talked about out loud to achieve solutions."

Demonstration projects showing that child abuse can be anticipated at birth and largely prevented, at least in its most serious forms, should encourage us to attack this problem. The millions of fearful and unhappy young people suffering abuse and the millions of maladjusted adults that result from this abuse are too great a price for us to continue to pay.

•　　　•　　　•　　　•

# CHILD ABUSE: A CASE STUDY

*Joel Steinberg and Hedda Nussbaum leave a Greenwich Village police station after being charged with Lisa's murder.*

On November 2, 1987, police discovered a battered and unconscious Lisa Steinberg, 6, on the floor of the Greenwich Village apartment where she lived. On November 3, doctors announced that Lisa had no brain activity. On November 4, they pronounced her brain dead. On November 5, just three days after being found and having never regained consciousness, Lisa Steinberg suffered a brain hemorrhage and died.

If the situation had been different, Lisa's sad story might have died with her. But Lisa had not been a child of poverty; rather, her adoptive father, Joel Steinberg, was a millionaire lawyer, living in an upscale New York City neighborhood. The knowledge that a nightmare such as this could happen in anyone's home, in anyone's community, shocked and horrified the nation.

The story that unfurled after little Lisa's death was almost too bizarre to believe. After Joel Steinberg and his live-in girlfriend, Hedda Nussbaum, were taken into custody it was disclosed that there had been another child in the apartment at the time. The child, 16-month-old Mitchell Steinberg, was discovered tied to a chair. Both children had been illegally adopted by Steinberg and lived with him and Nussbaum in the Greenwich Village apartment. Police searching the apartment later discovered evidence of drugs, an unloaded gun, and a blood-stained exercise bar.

After the story was made public, both natural mothers came forward; Mitchell's to reclaim her child, Lisa's to bury hers. Both women admitted that they had been unwed teenage mothers at the time of their child's birth, and each had made arrangements to have their baby placed in a good home. Mitchell's mother, Nicole Smigiel, claims she gave her baby to obstetrician Peter Sarosi to place. Sarosi later pleaded guilty to charges of illegally placing the infant with Steinberg and was given three year's probation. Lisa's mother, Michele Launders, paid Steinberg $500 to secure a good home for her daughter. Instead, Steinberg took the child home to his apartment.

On November 6, Joel Steinberg was indicted for murder, a charge to which he pleaded innocent. Although it was assumed that Nussbaum would also be arraigned, no indictment was sought against her. In October 1988, the prosecutors decided not to press charges against Nussbaum in return for her testimony against Steinberg. (Many people felt that, because of her own extensive injuries, Nussbaum was incapable of striking the fatal blow to Lisa.) At the trial, which began in October, Nussbaum testified that she and the children were repeatedly beaten, forced to eat hot peppers, and subjected to mind control (Steinberg attempted to hypnotize Nussbaum on several occasions and beat Lisa severely when he felt she was "staring" at him too much). Stories of drug abuse and psychological torment came to light as Nussbaum painted a picture of a controlling, sadistic man.

Tragically, the trial also revealed that several people, including friends, neighbors, and teachers, had noticed signs of abuse but had done little or nothing to interfere. The only person who had apparently spoken up was a student teacher whose observations were ignored.

On January 30, 1989, after months of testimony, the jury found Joel Steinberg guilty of first-degree manslaughter, stating they believed he had intended to hurt Lisa. On March 24, Steinberg was sentenced to the maximum prison term and a fine of $5,000 by Manhattan Supreme Court justice Harold Rothwax. This

*Lisa Steinberg's coffin is carried out of the funeral home.*

means that Steinberg will serve a maximum of 25 years. If paroled for good behavior, he could be released in seven years. (He had already served 16 months in jail prior to his sentencing.) Justice Rothwax, however, strenuously recommended that no parole be granted.

At the time of this printing, Steinberg's lawyers were preparing an appeal.

•　　　•　　　•　　　•

# APPENDIX:
# FOR MORE INFORMATION

The following national associations and organizations can provide general information about child abuse and where to go for help. They can also provide names and phone numbers of local treatment centers, as well as further information regarding how to report a suspected case of child abuse.

Action for Child Protection
211 East Blvd., Suite 2
Charlotte, NC 28203
(704) 332-1030

Adam Walsh Child Resource Center
1876 North University Drive,
   Suite 306
Ft. Lauderdale, FL 33322
(305) 475-4847

American Association for Protecting
   Children
9725 East Hampton Avenue
Denver, CO 80231
(303) 695-0811

American Public Welfare
   Association
810 First Street NE
Washington, DC 20002
(202) 293-7550

Child Welfare League of America
440 First Street NW
Washington, DC 20001
(202) 638-2952

Childhelp U.S.A., Inc.
6463 Independence Avenue
Woodland Hills, CA 91370
(818) 347-7280
hot line: (800) 422-4453

Children's Defense Fund
122 C Street NW
Washington, DC 20001
(202) 628-8787

Children's Institute International
711 South New Hampshire
Los Angeles, CA 90005
(213) 385-5100

Children's Rights of America
12551 Indian Rocks Road, Suite 11
Largo, FL 33544
(813) 593-0090

Defense for Children International
534 Eighth Street
Brooklyn, NY 11215
(718) 965-0245

Family Resource Coalition
230 North Michigan Avenue,
   Suite 1625
Chicago, IL 60601
(312) 726-4750

Find the Children
11811 West Olympic Blvd.
Los Angeles, CA 90064
(213) 477-6721

Institute for the Community as
Extended Family
P.O. Box 952
San Jose, CA 95108
(408) 280-5055

International Institute of Children's
Nature and Their Rights
1615 Myrtle Street NW
Washington, DC 20012
(202) 726-3341

C. Henry Kempe National Center
for the Prevention and Treatment
of Child Abuse and Neglect
1205 Oneida Street
Denver, CO 80220
(303) 321-3963

Missing Children of America
P.O. Box 10-1938
Anchorage, AK 99510
(907) 248-7300

Missing Children...Help Center
410 Ware Blvd., Suite 400
Tampa, FL 33619
(813) 623-5437

National Alliance for the Prevention
and Treatment of Child Abuse
c/o New York Foundling Hospital
1175 Third Avenue
New York, NY 10021
(212) 633-9300

National Assault Prevention Center
P.O. Box 02005
Columbus, OH 43202
(614) 291-2540

National Association of Counsel
for Children
1205 Oneida St.
Denver, CO 80220
(303) 321-3963

National Center on Child
Abuse and Neglect
P.O. Box 1182
Washington, DC 20013
(202) 245-2856

National Center for Missing and
Exploited Children
1835 K Street NW, Suite 600
Washington, DC 20006
(202) 634-9821

National Center for the Prosecution
of Child Abuse
1033 North Fairfax Street,
Suite 200
Alexandria, VA 22314
(703) 739-0321

National Committee for Prevention
of Child Abuse
332 South Michigan Avenue,
Suite 950
Chicago, IL 60604
(312) 663-3520

National Council on Child Abuse
and Family Violence
hot line: (800) 222-2000

National Court Appointed Special
Advocates Association
909 N.E. 43rd Street, Suite 202
Seattle, WA 98102
(206) 547-1059

National Exchange Club Foundation
for the Prevention of Child Abuse
3050 Central Avenue
Toledo, OH 43606
(419) 535-3232

Parents Against Molesters
P.O. Box 3357
Portsmouth, VA 23701
(804) 465-1582

Parents Anonymous
6733 South Sepulveda Blvd.,
Suite 270
Los Angeles, CA 90045
(800) 421-0353

# FURTHER READING

Altemeier, William A. III, M.D., Susan O'Connor, M.D., Peter M. Vietze, et al. "Antecedents of Child Abuse." *Journal of Pediatrics* 100 (1982): 823–29.

Bachmann, Gloria, M.D., et al. "Childhood Sexual Abuse and the Consequences in Adult Women." *Obstetrics and Gynecology* (April 1988): 631–42.

Caffey, John, M.D. "The Whiplash Shaken Infant Syndrome: Manual Shaking by the Extremities with Whiplash-Induced Intracranial and Intraocular Bleedings, Linked with Residual Permanent Brain Damage and Mental Retardation." *Pediatrics* 54 (October 1974): 396–403.

Canadian Medical Association Council on Health Care. "Family Violence: Guidelines for Recognition and Management." *Canadian Medical Association Journal* 132 (March 1, 1985): 541–53.

Chadwick, David, M.D. "Child Abuse." *Journal of the American Medical Association* 235 (May 3, 1976): 2017–18.

Christoffel, Katherine K., et al. "Epidemiology of Fatal Child Abuse: International Mortality Data." *Journal of Chronic Diseases* 34 (1981): 57–64.

Cohn, Anne Harris, and Deborah Daro. "Is Treatment Too Late: What Ten Years of Evaluative Research Tells Us." *Child Abuse and Neglect* 11 (1987): 433–42.

Crewdson, John. *By Silence Betrayed: Sexual Abuse of Children in America*. Boston: Little, Brown, 1988.

Daro, Deborah. *Confronting Child Abuse*. New York: Free Press, 1988.

Dziech, Billie Wright, and Charles B. Schudson. *On Trial: America's Courts and Their Treatment of Sexually Abused Children*. Boston: Beacon Press, 1989.

Frodi, Ann. "Contribution of Infant Characteristics to Child Abuse." *American Journal of Mental Deficiency* 85 (1981): 341–49.

Goldin, Harrison J. "For a New York City Department for Children." *New York Times*, December 5, 1987.

Goldstein, Joseph, Anna Freud, and Albert J. Solnit. *Beyond the Best Interest of the Child*. New York: Free Press, 1973.

Hakins, Paula. *Children at Risk*. Bethesda, MD: Adler and Adler, 1986.

Heins, Marilyn, M.D. "The 'Battered Child' Revisited." *Journal of the American Medical Association* 251 (June 22, 1984): 3295–3300.

Helfer, Ray E., M.D. "Where to Now, Henry?" *Pediatrics* 76 (December 1985): 993–97.

Helfer, Ray E., M.D., and Ruth S. Kempe, M.D., eds. *The Battered Child*. 4th ed. Chicago: University of Chicago Press, 1987.

Hight, Donald W., M.D., Harriet R. Bakalar, and James R. Lloyd, M.D. "Inflicted Burns in Children." *Journal of the American Medical Association* 242 (August 10, 1979): 517–20.

Jason, Janine, M. D. "Child Homicide Spectrum." *American Journal of Diseases of Children* 137 (1983): 578–81.

Joyner, G. "False Accusation of Child Abuse—Could It Happen To You?" *Women's Day*, May 1986.

Kempe, C. Henry, M.D. "Approaches to Preventing Child Abuse." *American Journal of Diseases of Children* 130 (September 1976): 941–47.

———. "Child Abuse—The Pediatrician's Role in Child Advocacy and Preventive Pediatrics." *American Journal of Diseases of Children* 132 (March 1978): 255–60.

———. "Sexual Abuse, Another Hidden Pediatric Problem." *Pediatrics* 62 (September 1978): 382–89.

Markham, Barbara. "Child Abuse Intervention: Conflicts in Current Practice and Legal Theory." *Pediatrics* 65 (January 1980): 180–85.

Newberger, Eli H., M.D., ed. *Child Abuse*. Boston: Little, Brown, 1982.

Newberger, Eli H., M.D., and Jessica H. Daniel. "Knowledge and Epidemiology of Child Abuse: A Critical Review of Concepts." *Pediatric Annals* (March 1976): 15–23.

Newberger, Eli H., M.D., and Robert L. Hampton. "Child Abuse Incidence and Reporting by Hospitals: Significance of Severity, Class, and Race." *American Journal of Public Health* 75 (January 1985): 56–60.

Newberger, Eli H., M.D., and Lesli Taylor. "Child Abuse in the International Year of the Child." *New England Journal of Medicine* 301 (November 29, 1979): 1205–12.

Rush, Florence. *The Best Kept Secret: Sexual Abuse of Children*. New York: McGraw-Hill, 1980.

Sgroi, Suzanne M., M.D. *A Handbook of Clinical Intervention in Child Sexual Abuse*. Lexington, MA: Lexington Books, 1982.

Smothers, Ronald. "In a Small Southern Town, a Church and Child Welfare Officials Do Battle." *New York Times*, June 16, 1988.

Staver, Sari. "In Wake of Sexual Abuse: Unraveling a Nightmare." *American Medical News*, March 22, 1985.

Unger, Judith. " 'Good' Mothers Feel Dark Urges." *New York Times*, May 10, 1988.

Wald, Michael, and P. Herbert Leiderman. *Protecting Abused and Neglected Children*. Palo Alto, CA: Stanford University Press, 1988.

Weiner, Irving B. "A Clinical Perspective on Incest." *American Journal of Diseases of Children* 132 (February 1978): 123–24.

# VIDEOTAPES

*Child Abuse: Physical and Behavioral Indicators; Sexually Misused Children: Identification, Documentation, Management; Helping the Abused Child.* Three 30-minute videotapes concerning various aspects of child abuse from the professional's viewpoint, these presentations are easily understandable and informative to the layperson as well. They are available for purchase from Media Library, University of Michigan Medical Center, 4440 Kresge 1, Box 56, Ann Arbor, Michigan 48109-0010; (313) 763-2074.

*Breaking Silence.* A one-hour film about two women who were sexually abused as children and had completely repressed the memories until adulthood as well as how one family is coping with the recently acknowledged fact that incest was part of its everyday life. Available for rental from Film Distribution Center, 1028 Industry Drive, Seattle, Washington, 98188; (206) 575-1575.

# GLOSSARY

**abandonment** to desert someone or something; the once-common and still not unheard of practice of leaving a child

**adolescence** the period of development between puberty and maturity, involving both psychological and physical growth

**anal intercourse** intercourse that involves the insertion of the penis into the anus

**child abuse** mental or physical harm inflicted on a child by an adult; includes external or internal bruises, fractures, wounds, burns, poisoning, or sexual molestation; also includes forms of neglect such as malnutrition and dehydration and failure to treat mental or physical ills that may impair growth and development

**emotional abuse** abuse of a child in the form of verbal insults, shouting, name-calling, and humiliation by an adult; emotional abuse may also encompass child neglect, which includes abandoning a child without adequate supervision or failing to provide adequate nutrition for a child

**exhibitionism** a psychological disorder in which a person becomes sexually aroused by exposing his or her genitals

**failure to thrive** a form of neglect seen in infants and caused by a lack of emotional nurturing from the mother; results in a cessation of growth, lethargy, or sickness in the child

**foster home** a home in which a child may be placed for a short period of time

**hemorrhage** a copious external or internal discharge of blood caused by a break in the wall of a blood vessel

**incest** sexual intercourse between persons so closely related that they are forbidden by law to marry

**indictment** a formal charge against a defendant, made as a result of the findings of a grand jury

**infanticide** the killing of infants; a practice that was common in ancient cultures such as those of China and Greece

**masturbation** stimulation of the genitals for sexual pleasure by means other than intercourse

**penetration** the act of forcing a way into; in the context of sexual intercourse, usually the insertion of the penis into the vagina or anus

**physical abuse** deliberately hitting, shaking, or otherwise harming a child's body

**pornography** films, pictures, or literature intended to arouse sexual excitement

**posttraumatic stress disorder** a chronic mental disorder that affects individuals who have been exposed to extreme stress or shock; symptoms include depression, chronic anxiety, outbursts of violent behavior, and inability to form close relationships

**prosecution** the legal procedure of bringing to trial and attempting to convict a person accused of a crime

**psychosis** mental disorder in which the patient loses touch with reality; symptoms include hallucinations, delusions, and agitated behavior

**rape** sexual intercourse without consent; employs the use of force, intimidation, or deception

**sexual abuse** sexual exploitation of a child; may include oral-genital contact between an adult and a child, touching a child's genitals, masturbation of the abuser by the child, exhibitionism of an adult in front of a child, and vaginal or anal intercourse

**urethra** a tube that carries urine from the bladder

**vaginal intercourse** intercourse usually involving the insertion of a man's penis into a woman's vagina

**venereal disease** infectious disease transmitted through sexual intercourse

**whiplash shaking syndrome** also known as "shaken baby syndrome"; bleeding in the brain of an infant caused by rapid and repeated shaking of the body; can lead to mental retardation, permanent brain damage, and/or blindness

# INDEX

## PICTURE CREDITS

**William A. Check** is the author of *Drugs of the Future* and *Drugs & Perception* in the Chelsea House ENCYCLOPEDIA OF PSYCHOACTIVE DRUGS, and *AIDS* and *Alzheimer's Disease* in the Chelsea House ENCYCLOPEDIA OF HEALTH. He holds a Ph.D. in microbiology from Case Western Reserve University. Dr. Check is also coauthor of *The Truth About Aids*, which won the American Medical Writer's Association Book Award, and a frequent contributor to medical reports for the National Institutes of Health and the Office of Technology Assessment.

**Solomon H. Snyder, M.D.,** is Distinguished Service Professor of Neuroscience, Pharmacology, and Psychiatry and director of the Department of Neuroscience at the Johns Hopkins University School of Medicine. He has served as president of the Society for Neuroscience and in 1978 received the Albert Lasker Award in Medical Research for his discovery of opiate receptors in the brain. Dr. Snyder is a member of the National Academy of Sciences and a Fellow of the American Academy of Arts and Sciences. He is the author of *Drugs and the Brain, Uses of Marijuana, Madness and the Brain, The Troubled Mind,* and *Biological Aspects of Mental Disorder.* He is also the general editor of Chelsea House's ENCYCLOPEDIA OF PSYCHOACTIVE DRUGS.

**C. Everett Koop, M.D., Sc.D.,** is Surgeon General, Deputy Assistant Secretary for Health, and Director of the Office of International Health of the U.S. Public Health Service. A pediatric surgeon with an international reputation, he was previously surgeon-in-chief of Children's Hospital of Philadelphia and professor of pediatric surgery and pediatrics at the University of Pennsylvania. Dr. Koop is the author of more than 175 articles and books on the practice of medicine. He has served as surgery editor of the *Journal of Clinical Pediatrics* and editor-in-chief of the *Journal of Pediatric Surgery.* Dr. Koop has received nine honorary degrees and numerous other awards, including the Denis Brown Gold Medal of the British Association of Paediatric Surgeons, the William E. Ladd Gold Medal of the American Academy of Pediatrics, and the Copernicus Medal of the Surgical Society of Poland. He is a Chevalier of the French Legion of Honor and a member of the Royal College of Surgeons, London.